How to Succeed as CEO of Your Life

Other Books by Paul Brownback

The Danger of Self-Love: Re-Examining a Popular Myth

Counterattack: Why Evangelicals are Losing the Culture War and How They Can Win

This is the Generation: Proof from Scripture that Christ Will Return in This Generation

How to Succeed as CEO of Your Life

12 Spiritual Principles I Wish I Had Learned Long Ago

Paul Brownback, PhD

FSP Foundation Stone Press

Dedication

To my children, Stephanie and Stephen,
who were great kids even through the years I was trying to learn
to succeed as CEO of my life.

Table of Contents

Acknowledgments

I would like to thank my dear wife, Connie, for giving good recommendations and proofing yet another book and for her willingness to live a widow's existence during the many hours I worked on it.

I also want to express special thanks to Don Otis, Publicist and President of Veritas Communications, for not only providing significant help but also extending remarkable patience and kindness.

Success is Achievable but not Guaranteed

Your Life Matters

It is difficult to imagine the feelings that gripped the heart of Adolf Hitler as he spent the day of April 30, 1945, in his "fuhrer-bunker." The previous day he had married Eva Braun, his mistress of many years. At around 3:30 he and Eva bit into thin glass vials of cyanide, after which Hitler shot himself in the head with a 7.65 mm Walther pistol. Though he may have attempted to delude himself regarding the impact of his decisions and behaviors, it would have been difficult even for him to escape the reality that he was terminating his life as an abject failure. Not only had the cause he led ended in ruin, but he also had presided over the murder of millions of innocent people and by his policies and initiatives caused the death of many millions more. He must have known that for centuries to come his name would be used as an epithet to depict humanity at its worst.

Compare his fate with the outcome of the life of William Wilberforce, who led the campaign that resulted in the Slavery Abolition Act 1833, which abolished slavery in most of the British Empire. Wilberforce died in peace just three days after hearing that the passage of the Act through Parliament was assured. He came to the conclusion of his life with confidence that he had invested it well.

Life confronts every human being with the prospects of success or failure. Contrary to the current cultural myth encapsulated in the words of Dodo Bird, "Everybody has won and all must have prizes," life offers no participation trophies, and some people do lose. A Christian song from a few decades ago declared, "In heaven's eyes there are no losers," but as we reflect on the lives of Judas Iscariot and Adolf Hitler we are gripped with the reality that life does have losers and with the possibility that we could be among them.

We tend, however, to ignore the prospect of winning or losing because life goes by so silently, like sand through an hourglass, that we can go for long stretches without ever reflecting on its passage, seldom thinking of it in its totality— what is my life amounting to? I have a friend who calculated the remaining weeks of his life using the actuary tables and then filled a large bowl with marbles, each representing one of those weeks. Every week he removes one marble to remind himself that life is passing by and to motivate himself to invest the resources God has given him effectively. Though we may not adopt this approach, it is nonetheless important that we maintain an awareness of the ephemeral nature of life and assess how well we are investing it.

Doing so is important for two reasons. First, your life comprises your most valuable possession. Jesus made this point, addressing the issue from the negative perspective, in Mark 8:36-37 where He asks rhetorically, "For what does it profit a man to gain the whole world and forfeit his soul? For what can a man give in return for his soul?" Because of the immeasurable value of our life, succeeding at life represents our most important objective.

How successfully we are investing our life is all the more crucial because we go through only once. We get no dry runs or second tries. We possess resources, are provided with opportunities, and get to make choices for one lifetime, and the results are forever etched in history as our legacy.

The underlying impetus for this book, however, resides in the reality that every one of us can succeed. It makes the case that God has not only appointed you as CEO of your life, but He has also provided you with all the resources necessary to succeed in that role. However, succeeding requires significant input on our part. Losing only requires that we do nothing. In fact, doing nothing will guarantee that outcome. In addition to our active engagement, success also requires that we concisely identify the commodity God calls us to produce and then apply the principles described in the chapters ahead in order to maximize the production of that commodity.

Foundation for Success

Foundational to succeeding as CEO of our lives is establishing a relationship with God, who owns the company. Because He designed the universe, success in life requires that our lives reflect that design. It is only as we acknowledge Him as owner and ultimate authority and seek to operate according to His design that we will manage our lives effectively. Doing so must begin with establishing a relationship with Him.

You can establish a relationship with God through a commitment of your life to Christ. If you have never made that commitment or are not sure what it entails, I would urge you at this point to turn to Appendix A, which provides more information on the topic.

Assessing Your Life as a Business

John Eckblad and David Kiel, wrote a book with the

evocative title *If Your Life Were a Business, Would You Invest in It?*[i] For many years I would have had to view my own life as a bad investment. Any honest assessment would have placed it in the junk bond category. I was failing to function effectively as its CEO.

I discovered that the greatest contributor to my past failures was a lack of clarity related to salient issues of life. Change has resulted from developing clarity regarding my role as CEO of my life, the commodity I am seeking to produce, and what I must do to optimize its production. Across the years the Lord has taught me principles that have helped me achieve clarity regarding these and related issues. Though my life continues to be a work in progress, I find that as I follow those principles I experience success.

Though I am grateful that I am on a better path today, I nonetheless regret those lost years, especially because of the resulting harm to others. I wish someone would have taught me the principles contained in this book before I had inflicted that damage. It is my heart's desire that these principles will enable you to avoid lost years and enjoy optimal success as CEO of your life.

Principle #1
Manage Proactively

Joe experienced both a jolt of excitement and a twinge of anxiety as for the first time he walked through the door of his new office. At age 42, he had earned an MBA and had worked in lesser management positions, but this was his first experience as CEO.

The excitement stemmed from the authority that the owners of ABC Widget Company invested in him. He relished the challenge of effectively managing company resources in order to make it successful. The anxiety arose from the related responsibility. The owners were counting on him to succeed.

Having spent the morning walking through the facility and meeting the employees, his plan for the afternoon was to meet with Bob, the Chief Operating Officer. Bob had been with the company from its inception 13 years earlier and had suffered through the previous five years of decline under the leadership of Oscar, the former CEO. Both the board and Bob himself realized that he was not CEO material but that he functioned at a high level as the Chief Operating Officer. In getting acquainted with him that morning, Joe sensed that he would serve as a great resource and consequently decided that a good starting point consisted of pursuing his input.

Joe began their meeting by asking Bob if he was acquainted with any short-term or long-term strategies that Oscar, the previous CEO, had employed. Bob's best efforts to conceal his frustration failed, and Joe immediately sensed his exasperation. Bob responded, "I never knew of or could detect any short-term or long-term strategies guiding Oscar's decision-making. Though Oscar was a nice person and was easy to work for, he just seemed to make decisions on the fly. If a machine broke, he would have the maintenance department repair it, and if it was beyond repair, he would buy a new one. But he seemed to have no systematic plan for maintaining and updating equipment. To my knowledge, he developed no marketing and sales programs. As sales declined, Oscar would occasionally give the sales department a pep talk, but he never initiated any plan for dealing with the problem systematically."

Bob vented his frustration for some time regarding the previous CEO's failure to proactively manage the company. Joe could tell that these emotions had been building for some time and for good reason. Had the board allowed Oscar to stay, in another year or two the company likely would have gone bankrupt. Bob's livelihood and that of the other employees required that Joe proactively manage the company in order to pull it out of its current malaise and move it into a profitable future. Without making any negative reference to Oscar, Joe shared with Bob his intention to employ an aggressive management approach in order to move the company forward. He caught the look of relief that crossed Bob's face.

Joe reflected on the difference between Oscar's management style and his own, if Oscar's approach could be categorized as management at all. He concluded that the distinction might best be described using the terms "reactive and "proactive." Oscar waited until needs arose and problems developed, and then he reacted to them. Joe preferred a proactive approach.

Joe identified two negative outcomes resulting from Oscar's reactive approach and noted the corresponding superiority of his proactive management style. First, Oscar's method constantly left the company on the brink of disaster. By putting off dealing with issues until they reached crisis level, each area rather than operating at peak performance was always hovering near the bottom of functionality. Equipment that did work was on the verge of breaking down and therefore did not function at peak efficiency. If sales were not at crisis level, they were never far from it. Joe's management approach would proactively employ the available resources in order to optimize the functionality of equipment, production, marketing, sales, and every other aspect of the operation.

Oscar's approach was also harmful because operating in crisis mode often resulted in spending more than necessary. Changing the oil in a piece of equipment, preventive maintenance, costs substantially less than fixing the machine after it breaks down. In addition, broken equipment slows down or stops production, which carries a high price tag.

Joe was committed to avoid Oscar's mistake of reactive management and instead to manage ABC Widget Company proactively in order to generate maximum profit.

You Are CEO of Your Life

Success at life begins by recognizing that God has assigned to us the role of CEO. A CEO, Chief Executive Officer, is a person given authority over resources by an owner or group of owners and then held responsible to use those resources to earn a profit. Consequently, authority and responsibility comprise the dominant aspects of the role of CEO.

Scripture teaches that God has assigned us the role of CEO of our lives using the term "stewardship." Stewardship is an archaic word for management. Churches tend to employ it primarily in relation to giving. However, the biblical concept of stewardship includes managing the full range of our assets in order to earn maximum profit for the Lord.

In biblical times, though a steward often was a slave, he nonetheless worked at an executive level. His master gave him authority over all his possessions and assigned him the corresponding responsibility to manage them for his optimal benefit. We see the parallel, then, between a steward in biblical times and a contemporary CEO. God has assigned us authority to make decisions regarding how we use our lives and holds us responsible to invest them to earn maximum profit for Him.

Several passages of Scripture convey this truth. For example, 1 Peter 4:10 directs, "As each one has received a gift, minister it to one another, as good stewards of the manifold grace of God." (NKJV). The "gift," i.e. the "manifold grace," refers to the full range of resources God has granted us. Peter calls us to be "good" stewards. The Greek word conveys the idea of excellence. We are to steward (manage) the package of gifts with which God has entrusted us with excellence, i.e. so as to advance God's agenda most effectively.

Our biblical role as steward differs from a contemporary CEO in that a CEO can quit, but we cannot. We cannot escape our responsibility as CEO of our lives. Every morning when we open our eyes, our authority over our package of resources and the related responsibilities confront us. We can neglect or ignore our management responsibilities, but we cannot escape them.

Nor can we delegate that responsibility to anyone else— "Let Harry take charge." And even if we could let Harry take charge, very soon we would want to take our management responsibilities back because we may not like some of Harry's decisions. Would you want Harry selecting your spouse or your job?

In addition, we cannot escape our management responsibilities for our life because they are inherent in our very existence. Every human being has a package of resources under his authority and the corresponding responsibility to invest them effectively. Like it or not, being human assigns to us management responsibilities. In large measure, that is what life is about.

Ultimately we cannot dodge our management responsibilities because we will give an account to the Lord for the job we do. The apostle Paul taught, "For we must all appear before the judgment seat of Christ, so that each one may receive what is due for what he has done in the body, whether good or evil." (2 Corinthians 5:10) Consequently, succeeding at life requires that we embrace that responsibility and aggressively work to fulfill it effectively.

This book identifies 12 principles that if implemented will enable you to succeed as CEO of the one life God has given you. I trust that you will embrace and employ them.

The Fun of Management

Though management of our lives constitutes an inescapable responsibility, we should not view our position as CEO negatively. Management can be fun. God created us to do this kind of work and to find pleasure and fulfillment in doing it. Humans tend to enjoy the challenge of making things work. Doing so gets our creative juices flowing. Some people enjoy putting ingredients together to make a great entree or dessert. Others get kicks out of transforming a pile of lumber into a treehouse. Others think assembling a bunch of components into a computer is fun, especially when they turn it on and it actually works. God has designed humans to enjoy taking authority over resources and transforming them into something meaningful.

The ultimate opportunity to express this natural bent toward management resides in functioning as CEO of our lives. It can be a special source of joy to shape the raw materials God has given us into a productive and meaningful life.

Management is not only fun because we enjoy the process, but also because we find the end result rewarding. It is fun to create and also to benefit from the fruits of our creation. We are blessed when people enjoy the recipes we put together, when the kids have fun in the treehouse, or when that computer we assembled writes and prints documents, enables us to read our email, or allows us to make drawings.

Viewing our responsibilities as CEO of our life as a source of drudgery will engender failure. Though managing our lives can be demanding, God assigned us this work as a means of fulfilling some of our deepest human needs—the need to create and organize. That is why God assigned Adam and Eve management responsibility for the Garden of Eden. Succeeding as CEO of our lives requires that we delight in this assignment. Approaching this role with enthusiasm will significantly increase our prospects for success.

Approaching our management responsibilities reactively, doing just enough to get by, will drain all the enjoyment out of fulfilling this role. As we proactively seek to organize every aspect of our lives and make them fully productive, both the process and the outcome will provide fun and satisfaction.

Management: the Essential Remedy for Chaos

If ABC Widget Company employed all skilled workers, why did it need a CEO? Why must we manage our lives? Perhaps we can best grasp the compelling need for management by considering the issue from the negative perspective. *Chaos is life's default setting.* In other words, to experience chaotic existence all we need to do is nothing—it just happens. Consequently, any aspect of our life that is not intentionally managed will descend into chaos.

This phenomenon manifests itself in our physical world as expressed by the Second Law of Thermodynamics, which states, "Entropy in a closed system increases." Entropy is merely a term expressing chaos, the opposite of order. A closed system is one that blocks the entry of an organizing force. Therefore, the Second Law of Thermodynamics merely states that a system left to itself tends toward chaos.

This tendency toward chaos also manifests itself in the human realm. We have all witnessed thriving companies go bankrupt because they ceased to be aggressively managed.

The Second Law of Thermodynamics makes reference to

increased chaos in a closed system. What about an open system, one in which energy is introduced? If we throw a stick of dynamite into a closed system, we introduce energy, but that energy only serves to increase the chaos. Reversing the chaos and bringing order requires intelligent energy.

Warding off chaos in our lives also requires intelligent energy, i.e. management. Our minds need to provide the intelligence to organize and our wills, activating the full range of our capabilities, provide the energy. That is the essence of management: our minds developing a plan that provides structure and our wills implementing that plan.

Because the default setting in life is chaos, every aspect of life requires management. Any element of life, big or small, left unmanaged will become chaotic and produce trouble. If I have a rare Saturday afternoon with nothing to do, and I fail to intentionally manage that block of time, chaos will rear its ugly head in the form of my eating too much, buying something I don't need, or my capitulation to some other form of chaotic living. Though we need relaxation, even that must be managed.

For humans, this tendency toward chaos comprises only one source of trouble. Scripture informs us that the world, the flesh, and the devil serve as catalysts that ramp up the production of chaos to especially destructive levels. The world is aggressively selling us a full range of commodities, telling us that we owe it to ourselves to buy them. The flesh gets into the act by craving those products, and the devil is active in convincing us that they will produce ultimate happiness that we can never experience without them. These sordid activities of the world, the flesh, and the devil make aggressive management of every aspect of our lives all the more imperative.

Some Human Beings Are More Proactive Than Others

Management, or its absence, becomes apparent as we consider the landscaping of the homes in most neighborhoods. Some people employ no landscaping strategy. Whatever is growing around their house was put there by the contractor when the house was built. If necessary, they mow the grass, which by now consists mainly of weeds. If a bush dies, they may remove it but give no thought to replacing it. By way of contrast, other homes reveal a landscaping plan that has produced an attractive yard. The presence or absence of management becomes obvious to the casual observer driving by.

My intention is not to speak ill of those who do not landscape their yards. They may have concluded that doing so does not constitute good stewardship of their time and money. However, landscaping our lives is essential and worth the investment. While the lives of some people reflect proactive planning, others, like Oscar, live a day at a time, putting out fires as they flare up.

The situations of life force everyone to manage their lives to some degree. If we do not mow our grass, sooner or later it becomes difficult to find the front door. The need for food and other necessities forces us to manage our money to some extent. Managing our lives in response to the pressures confronting us comprises a reactive approach. The person taking a proactive approach prepares and follows a budget, devises a program for caring for his health, and takes initiative to organize the other areas of his life.

One difference between these two styles of management, as Joe concluded, is that the reactive approach keeps the individual functioning at a crisis level. Since he does not act until disaster threatens, every area of his life hovers barely over the breaking point, resulting in life at the lowest levels of existence. Not acting until he encounters a medical crisis tends to leave him in poor health. Waiting until he runs out of money in the middle of the month leaves his finances in disarray. Not tending to his relationships, not maintaining his home, and not intentionally organizing other components of his life at best results in an existence barely above the chaos level. Because the proactive person develops and implements initiatives to manage the various components of life, he functions at a high level of existence.

The crises created by a reactive approach waste time, energy, and money, which leads to further crises. The proactive approach, on the other hand, tends to avoid most disasters, leaving the individual and family with more resources with which to optimize life. For example, the person who does not maintain his car makes himself vulnerable to a breakdown on the road or even an accident, either outcome soaking up a lot of resources and adding to the chaos of his life. The proactive person who maintains his vehicle will avoid most of those problems. A proactive approach promotes stable, organized, and productive lives and protects our resources.

It seems that human beings may fall along a continuum, perhaps following a bell curve, with some persons more inclined to take a reactive approach to managing their lives while others tend toward being proactive. If you are not wired toward proactively managing your life, that is not a put-down. We all have our inclinations in different directions. However, not being inclined toward proactivity makes it all the more essential that you intentionally work at it, because succeeding as CEO of your life depends on it.

Even if you tend to be more proactive, chances are that in some areas of life you are more reactive. I know some men who manage proactively at work but take a reactive approach at home. Just ask their wives. Some people are proactive in caring for their homes but reactive in caring for their health. All of us seem to have areas that call for increased proactive management.

A study of the ministries of Jesus and Paul, the lives most extensively described in the New Testament, reveals that both intentionally managed their ministries. New Testament scholars tracing the steps of Jesus detect a plan for covering certain territories, for training His disciples, and for pursuing other objectives.

In Romans 15:19, Paul in describing his ministry notes that "from Jerusalem and all the way around to Illyricum I have fulfilled the ministry of the gospel of Christ." This reference to his geographical progression from Jerusalem to Illyricum, modern-day Albania and Croatia, together with his assertion a few verses later that he planned to visit the church in Rome on his way to Spain, suggests that he was implementing a ministry plan.

Likewise, our success requires management of every aspect of our lives. I would encourage you to circle a number on the line below, or at least select one in your mind, that reflects the extent to which you see yourself proactively managing your life.

Reactive>> 1 2 3 4 5 6 7 8 9 10 <<Proactive

It might also be helpful to ask your spouse or a good friend to identify where he or she perceives that you fall along this spectrum. A comparison might be revealing. Another good exercise would be to rate three areas of your life in which you are least proactive.

History of Failure

As I noted earlier, during my younger years I failed to grasp my responsibility to manage my life. No identifiable plan guided my decisions, large or small. Only much later did I begin to recognize my management responsibilities. For whatever reason, it never occurred to me that God had assigned me the role of CEO of my life. My management approach paralleled Oscar's and produced a similar outcome. The resulting lack of management led to entropy, chaos, and failure.

I was not trying to be a bad person. A CEO does not have to try to be bad to ruin a company. Oscar seems to have been a good person. I kept my life in chaos merely by failing to proactively manage it.

This reality was tragic on numerous counts. First, I was raised in a Christian home, and therefore I had exposure to biblical truth. This outcome was even more tragic because I had made a commitment to Christ at a young age and in some respects had adopted a biblical lifestyle. However, I never grasped the part of the message about God assigning me the role as CEO of my life and the related responsibility to intentionally manage it. Maybe it had been conveyed to me. If so, I didn't hear it. Maybe I should have figured it out for myself, but I didn't. Whatever understanding of that obligation

I did possess was too vague to challenge me regarding my failures and to motivate me to change my ways.

When I finally woke up to my biblical responsibilities and my failure to meet them, it was impossible to undo the wasted years. Those failures left me with deep regrets regarding missed opportunities, joys, and fulfillment. Even greater remorse resulted from the realization that my unmanaged life had hurt others. Moving through life without a clear purpose and the drive to achieve that purpose left me like a ship cut loose in a harbor, banging into other ships in the vicinity, inflicting substantial damage.

My desire to help individuals avoid similar regrets over wasted years and hurt to others comprises the driving force behind this book. I am convinced that even many Christians are not managing their lives intentionally and optimally because they are not consciously aware that God has assigned them the role of CEO of their lives.

Succeeding at life begins with embracing and engaging in our role as CEO. I would encourage you to reflect on whether you have embraced your role as CEO of your life and are intentionally and proactively working to meet the related responsibilities. If not, I would challenge you to take a minute now and commit yourself to that role. As you do, and as you apply the principles described in this book for succeeding at that role, you will discover the enjoyment that flows from fulfilling your responsibilities as CEO of your life and the overwhelming array of benefits that result.

Embracing this role prompts us to ask, What is the nature of the commodity God has called us to produce? The chapter ahead addresses that issue.

Principle #2
Identify the Product

In managing ABC Widget Company, Joe knew that he had to maintain one ultimate priority: the design, production, and sales of widgets. Joe had queried the board on considering the production of commodities other than widgets, but they were committed to staying with the product line stated in the company name. Consequently, widget design, production, and sales offered the company's only source of profit.

Joe had never before worked at a company that produced widgets. Therefore, he had no in-depth knowledge regarding their nature or expertise regarding how to produce them. Of course, he had a casual acquaintance, having seen and even used them at times, but he had no in-depth exposure to the wide variety of widget shapes, sizes, and styles. He realized that to be effective as CEO of ABC Widget Company he would need to familiarize himself thoroughly with the essential qualities of widgets and the various forms they could take so that he could determine which ones would generate the most profit for the company and how to best produce them.

What Business Are We In?

In their book, *If Your Life Were a Business Would You Invest in It?* Eckblad and Kiel report:

> Successful businesses identify and concentrate on what is essential to the enterprise and they spend a great deal of time focusing on the question, "What businesses are we really in?"[ii]

What business are we in? As CEO of our lives, what commodity has God called us to produce? Success requires that we discover the nature of that product.

Christ identifies that commodity by defining the First and Second Great Commandments as follows:

> And one of them, a lawyer, asked him a question to test him. "Teacher, which is the great commandment in the Law?" And he said to him, "You shall love the Lord your God with all your heart and with all your soul and with all your mind. This is the great and first commandment. And a second is like it: You shall love your neighbor as yourself. On these two commandments depend all the Law and the Prophets." (Matthew 22:35-40)

The Greek term for love in this passage is agape. Jesus in effect is telling us that our job as human beings, as believers, is to produce agape. He further accentuates this job description by asserting that the production of agape embodies all the teachings of the Law and Prophets. In addition, Jesus established agape production as our job when issuing the New Commandment to His disciples: "A new commandment I give to you, that you love one another: just as I have loved you, you also are to love one another." (John 13:34).

The apostle Paul highlights the significance of agape in Romans 13:8-9:

> Owe no one anything, except to love each other, for the one who loves another has fulfilled the law. For the commandments, "You shall not commit adultery, You shall not murder, You shall not steal, You shall not covet," and any other commandment, are summed up in this word: "You shall love your neighbor as yourself."

Paul makes the same point even more succinctly in Galatians 5:14: "For the whole law is fulfilled in one word: 'You shall love your neighbor as yourself.'"

Paul accentuates the centrality of agape in 1 Corinthians 13, the love chapter. In that passage he in essence asserts that if our lives are characterized by agape we are achieving the purpose God assigned to us, and if they are not, we are failing, regardless of how altruistic our deeds appear to be.

The New Testament underscores the primacy of agape production by the frequency with which it is mentioned. The noun form of agape appears 117 times in the New Testament and the verb form occurs 144 times. Not only are these terms found frequently, but they are used in critical passages, demonstrating that agape constitutes the central theme of Scripture.

Scripture promotes agape not only in verses that use the term but also in countless other passages that describe, command, and illustrate agape. For example, Jesus tells the story of the Good Samaritan to illustrate His teaching on love, and yet the story never once uses the term agape.

The factors cited above confirm that agape comprises the commodity God calls us to produce. In other words, *God has commissioned you as CEO of Agape Incorporated.* God designed human beings to be *agape producing organisms.* That represents the ultimate purpose for our existence. Therefore, success as a human being entails eliminating selfish, i.e. anti-agape, tendencies and instead managing our lives to maximize agape production.

The Specific Nature of this Commodity

Defining love can be challenging because while Greek has several words that refer to different types of love, English is limited to one. Agape refers to intentions and the corresponding actions designed to benefit others. Philia describes affection, emotional love, which can cover a broad range of feelings from friendship to romance. Eros denotes sexual love.

Since the English word "love" covers all of these, it is often difficult to identify the type of love a person using the term has in mind. In our feelings-saturated society, even when people are talking about agape, they tend to allow their thinking and communication to slip away from the intentions and actions of agape toward the feelings-orientation of philia. Often this unintended and undetected transition in meaning from agape to philia occurs in the middle of a conversation or even a single sentence. Such unwitting replacement of agape with philia leads to confusion.

Let me clarify the difference between agape and philia. Jesus calls us to display agape toward our enemies. We cannot make ourselves feel warmly toward enemies (philia), but we can seek their benefit (agape). Suppose a coworker snubs you and treats you rudely. Try as you might, you cannot conjure up warm feelings (philia) toward this coworker. You learn, though, that she is about to get fired because she lacks an understanding of a certain aspect of her job that you know well and could teach her. Despite your negative feelings (lack of philia), you offer to help her get up to speed in that area (an expression of agape).

As an aside, often a display of agape toward another person engenders philia. We tend to develop warm feelings for those we are helping, even overcoming previous animosity. I had a student who was struggling with negative feelings toward a relative who had treated her badly. She wanted to rid herself of those feelings but did not know how. I encouraged her to think of some kindness (agape) she might do for that person. She decided to buy her a gift. Later she shared with me that it had worked, that doing an act of kindness toward this relative had eradicated her negative feelings. Consequently, the focus on agape does not neglect philia but actually promotes it.

Agape and Unconditional Love

In contemporary evangelical circles, the mention of agape love tends to elicit the response, "Oh, I know what that is. Agape is unconditional love." Because agape is central to our topic and because this is currently such a widespread perspective, it is necessary for us to examine this definition.

Those using the term unconditional love seem to mean that we should seek to benefit others regardless of their attitude or actions toward us. This perspective is valid as far as it goes. In displaying agape our interest is benefiting the other person and is not conditioned on how they treat us.

Though extending agape should not be conditioned on what we get in return, other considerations do call for the establishment of conditions. Evangelicals frequently speak of the need to establish *boundaries*. The term boundaries is just another word for conditions. Without realizing it, they are asserting that the proper functioning of any relationship requires conditions. For example, God established the condition of fidelity as a basis for marriage. This recognition of the need for boundaries reveals their awareness that an "unconditional" approach to relationships cannot work, but that reality requires establishing boundaries, i.e. conditions.

The term "unconditional love" is not found in Scripture but comes from secular psychology. The related psychological theory loads agape with a substantial amount of unscriptural baggage that can skew our understanding of it. I address the problems of equating agape with "unconditional love" in detail in my book, *Counterattack: Why Evangelicals Are Losing the Culture War and How They Can Win.* In this book I will limit my analysis to the following two observations.

First, in displaying agape we must consider all those people affected and not just the individual whom we are seeking to benefit. For example, a judge showing leniency to a repeated sex offender is not displaying agape toward future victims or society as a whole. Therefore, one condition for displaying agape resides in protecting the welfare of others besides the person toward whom we are seeking to display agape. This condition comes into play more often than we might realize. Some evangelicals advocate displaying agape by allowing illegal immigrants to enter our country. The decision to show agape toward them, however, must be conditioned on its impact on the citizens of our country such as the influx of crime and disease. Unconditional love does not consider those issues, but they deserve consideration.

Another factor calling for conditions in the display of agape has to do with the reality that we possess limited resources. For example, money is a major resource for displaying agape. However, since our supply of money is limited, we can only show agape, extend benefit, to a limited number of people. Consequently, a condition for investing our resources entails identifying the person who comprises the best investment.

For example, you want to help a needy person. Of two unemployed persons under consideration, the one seeking to find a job seems to be the better investment. A person may respond, "But I still love them both," by which they are referring to feelings, confusing agape and philia. You are actually showing agape, providing monetary benefit, only to one of these two people.

These factors demonstrate that it is not valid to apply the term "unconditional love" to agape. Rather, it is best to define agape simply as seeking the benefit of others.

Keeping the First Commandment First

It is strange but true that in seeking to produce agape it is easy for us to overlook the First Commandment. We tend to think of benefiting needy human beings while overlooking loving God. Perhaps we are inclined to omit God in our plans for agape production because agape entails benefiting others, and we think of God as having everything. Therefore, we conclude that we cannot do anything that would benefit Him. Since Scripture positions loving God as the First Commandment, apparently we can benefit God.

What can we do for God? We can bring joy to the heart of God by worship, obedience, and loving others. We can be a blessing to God by representing Him well before a watching world. Parents can relate to this. It brings joy to our hearts as our children honor us, obey us, get along with one another, and represent us well by their lives.

We can detect in God's conversation with Satan the joy that the righteous lifestyle of Job brought to His heart.

> And the LORD said to Satan, "Have you considered my servant Job, that there is none like him on the earth, a blameless and upright man, who fears God and turns away from evil?" (Job 1:8)

Hebrews 11:5 records God's pleasure in observing the life of Enoch:

> By faith Enoch was taken up so that he should not see death, and he was not found, because God had taken him. Now before he was taken he was commended as having pleased God.

Scripture indicates that our giving brings pleasure to God:

> I have received full payment, and more. I am well supplied, having received from Epaphroditus the gifts you sent, a fragrant offering, a sacrifice acceptable and pleasing to God. (Philippians 4:18)

Other passages also reveal that our godly living and sacrificial service bring joy to the heart of God. In contrast, Scripture indicates that ungodly living causes God grief:

> The LORD saw that the wickedness of man was great in the earth, and that every intention of the thoughts of his heart was only evil continually. And the

LORD regretted that he had made man on the earth, and it grieved him to his heart. (Genesis 6:5-6)

It seems that God is especially pleased when we love one another. Parents quickly get frustrated when their children fight and experience substantial joy when they observe their children being kind to one another.

The joy we bring to God by loving our neighbor reveals the connection between the first and second commandments. After describing the First Commandment, the mandate to love God, Jesus says, "And a second is like it: You shall love your neighbor as yourself." (Matthew 22:39) By saying "a second is like it," Jesus indicates that loving our neighbor is like, related to, loving God. We show our love for God primarily by loving our neighbor.

Understanding this connection between the First and Second Commandments is crucial because the First Commandment provides the framework for the Second. We keep the First Commandment by loving people in accordance with God's directions.

In contemporary society we hear people asserting that we must embrace all forms of "love." However, not everything our society labels as "love" is compatible with God's commandments. This contemporary perspective on loving others ignores the First Commandment. It is essential that we keep the First Commandment first, and make the Second Commandment subservient to it. Only as we fulfill the Second Commandment within the guidelines of the First will we bring joy to the heart of God.

Levels of Agape

We display agape at two levels: morality and grace. Understanding agape requires a working knowledge of these levels of agape production and their relationship.

Morality

Morality entails giving others what we owe them, that is, dealing with them fairly and honestly. This also includes the negative—*not* treating others in harmful ways they do not deserve such as taking their possessions or hurting them physically. Synonyms might include fairness, righteousness, and ethical behavior.

We tend not to think of morality as a form of agape, but it is. Being fair and honest is more loving than being unfair and dishonest. A just society is more loving than an unjust one. The Apostle Paul draws the connection between morality and agape in Romans 13:9-10: "For the commandments, 'You shall not commit adultery, you shall not murder, you shall not steal, you shall not covet,' and any other commandment, are summed up in this word: 'You shall love your neighbor as yourself.'"

Since agape entails seeking the benefit of others, morality—giving them what we owe them—constitutes its foundational level. Loving them requires that we benefit them at least to that extent.

Morality serves as the gears that make society work. Government, business, family, educational institutions, and interaction between neighbors and friends all depend on the exercise of morality. For example, it is virtually impossible to maintain a good relationship with a person who lies or steals. The absence of morality results in relational chaos and disintegration.

We can see how immoral behaviors such as murder, stealing, and the like fail to display agape. But what about sexual behaviors such as cohabitation and homosexuality? If these relationships are consensual, in what way do they deprive others of their just due and are therefore unloving?

As noted earlier, the First Commandment requires that we love God. Maintaining His moral instructions regarding sexuality comprises love toward Him—love on the vertical plane. Disregard for His instructions is acting in an unloving way toward Him.

On the horizontal plane, maintaining God's moral

standards produces agape because they provide the greatest benefit to others, though that outcome is not always evident to us. It is obvious, however, in most cases. For example, cohabitation fails to provide the lifetime commitment commensurate with sexual intimacy. Thus, even though sexual relations are consensual, failure to make that commitment takes something very precious from persons without giving them due compensation. This arrangement also robs children born into that relationship of the stable home life parents owe them and marriage provides.

Grace

While morality comprises the foundational level of agape, grace constitutes its highest expression. We have defined morality as giving others what we owe them. Grace consists of giving others what we do not owe them. This also includes forgiveness—not exacting from them what they owe us.

Your neighbor is sick, so you mow his lawn. You have no moral obligation to do so. Therefore, this action represents an act of grace, going beyond what you owe. Giving to charities embodies grace. The cross exhibits history's greatest expression of grace—Christ's dying for our sins, providing us with forgiveness, eternal life, and countless other blessings He did not owe us and we do not deserve.

While morality serves as the gears that make society work, grace provides the oil that lubricates those gears, which reduces friction and prevents overheating. If we were all perfect, we could do just fine in a society characterized solely by morality. Because of human flaws, however, we need the oil of grace to keep relationships and society running smoothly.

Most of us have overdrawn our checking account, resulting in brutal fees of $35 or more for each bounced check. Our agreement with the bank gives it the moral right to charge those fees. Then banks introduced overdraft protection, grace that supplies oil to the financial gears. Grace is the overdraft protection that God extends to human beings and that God calls us to extend to our spouses, children, friends, and even our enemies.

The Relationship between Morality and Grace

Because morality comprises the foundational level of agape, it is wrong to extend grace at the expense of morality, e.g. to neglect paying my electric bill in order to give to a charity. Doing so in essence is stealing from the electric company to help others. Agape requires that we meet our moral obligations first. We must pay creditors what we owe them before giving others what we do not owe them.

If we do not maintain morality as the required foundation for agape, instead displaying grace at the expense of morality, our individual lives and society will quickly descend into chaos, inflicting harm on everyone. The gears of society will cease to operate properly, leaving a puddle of the oil of grace on the floor.

Maintaining morality while extending grace requires that someone must pay for grace. The cross provides the ultimate example of this principle. God did not provide grace, forgiveness for our sins, by sweeping them under the carpet. That would have been unjust—grace at the expense of morality. Rather, He paid for them on the cross. Grace comes at a cost. The Good Samaritan's display of grace cost him effort, time, and financial resources. Mowing my neighbor's lawn as an act of grace demands my time and energy.

The Apostle Paul instructed, "Let the thief no longer steal, but rather let him labor, doing honest work with his own hands, so that he may have something to share with anyone in need." (Ephesians 4:28) Paul required that this man earn the resources necessary to manifest grace. When we display grace, we must be willing to pay the price.

God calls us to produce agape. This chapter has revealed that producing it effectively can be more complex than it might appear at first blush, requiring that we familiarize ourselves its nature and develop skill in its application. What opportunities does life provide for displaying agape? The next chapter examines the scope of those possibilities.

Principle #3
Produce Agape by All Means

As Joe tried to get his arms around the whole field of widget production, he realized that it encompassed more territory than he initially imagined. He thought about the various types of widgets and the prospects of developing new ones in the future. His mind also went to the broad range of equipment available for their production. He realized that he could produce them in-house or outsource part or all of their production. It also dawned on him that though some aspects of the operation, such as accounting, though not engaged directly in producing widgets, nonetheless comprised essential pieces of the process. Likewise, activities such as research and development and training new employees or current employees on new equipment did not directly produce widgets, but they were nonetheless indispensable for their production.

As Joe contemplated all of these factors, he realized that producing widgets encompassed a broader scope than he had previously thought.

The Scope of Agape

Perhaps the most comprehensive command in all of Scripture, the one encompassing the broadest scope, resides in the apostle Paul's terse mandate "Let all that you do be done in love." (1 Corinthians 16:14 NASB) This command connotes that everything we do can and should be designed to produce agape, i.e. benefit others.

It is difficult to get our minds around the far-reaching implications of this verse. In fact, it is easy just to let it go over our heads, to view it as a great motto for a Hobby Lobby wall plaque, which it would be, without coming to grips with its immense implications for our lives and the overwhelming impact it would have if we applied it.

To enable us to envision the reach of this command, it is helpful to consider the two predominant forms in which we produce agape: 1) being the person God designed us to be; 2) doing the tasks God designed us to do. Those two aspects of our lives encompass virtually everything about us. If we would consistently display agape in both of these areas, we would be maintaining Paul's mandate to reflect love through every aspect of our existence.

Being the Person God Designed Us to Be

We can provide great benefit to others merely by displaying loving personality traits. The Fruit of the Spirit described by the apostle Paul embodies those traits: "But the fruit of the Spirit is love, joy, peace, patience, kindness, goodness, faithfulness, gentleness, self-control...." (Galatians 5:22-23)

Since the word "fruit" related to the Fruit of the Spirit is singular, some Bible scholars have speculated that Paul is describing a singular, integrated commodity. Because the first characteristic on this list is love, agape, they have concluded that agape constitutes the singular fruit in view, and that the other eight aspects of this fruit comprise different expressions of agape. In other words, the Fruit of the Spirit is like an orange. Though it is one piece of fruit, as we remove the peel we discover that it is comprised of different segments. This seems to be a valid understanding of the Fruit of the Spirit, especially when we consider that the other eight characteristics comprise expressions of agape. For example, being patient is an expression of agape while impatience is selfish. Other New Testament passages describe additional personality traits that convey agape.

Persons abounding with the Fruit of the Spirit extend agape to virtually every life they touch. In a recent discussion with a friend from Alaska, he mentioned the tremendous difficulty people moving to that part of the world have in adjusting to the lack of sunshine during the dark months. Even those in Seattle tend to get depressed by the many overcast days. Likewise, human beings struggle in an environment devoid of the sunshine of agape. Being around impatient, ungracious people, individuals that fail to radiate the sunshine of the Fruit of the Spirit, can wear on and depress us, but interacting with people exuding a godly personality is encouraging and uplifting.

It may seem strange that joy is listed as an expression of agape. However, much time spent around a grumpy person quickly reveals the blessing of living in an environment abounding in joy. A joyful personality benefits all those coming in contact with it, lifting their spirits and brightening their day. The same might be said of peace. Interaction with an individual whose life is constantly in turmoil can be wearing, while a person who exudes tranquility produces an environment that reduces stress and promotes a sense of well-being.

Perhaps the display of the Fruit of the Spirit makes its greatest impact in the family setting. Within that venue it pours out many wonderful blessings. Living with a person overflowing with the Fruit of the Spirit makes marriage a joy and brings countless blessings to children.

The Fruit of the Spirit also provides a significant benefit through what it filters out. The presence of the Fruit of the Spirit eliminates qualities antithetical to it such as cursing, drunkenness, drugs, anger, infidelity, dishonesty, and selfishness. When people enter homes permeated with the Fruit of the Spirit, they can sense God's love in the atmosphere.

The same benefits of agape exists everywhere the person projecting the Fruit of Spirit is present. Recently Jessica took a new job. When she entered the office she could feel the darkness. As she began to display the light, life, and love of Christ in that loveless and joyless place, the people working there noticed a difference in the entire atmosphere. Even believers who had allowed the darkness to suppress their light started to come out of the shadows and began to shine. Though the environment in this office continues to be a work in progress, the agape emanating from Jessica is transforming this workplace.

Though current laws and policies in public schools and universities restrict Christian teachers from overt ministry, their display of the Fruit of the Spirit makes all the difference in the classroom, the faculty lounge, and on campus. Likewise, Christian politicians that carry the Fruit of the Spirit into government can exercise a transforming influence on society through honesty, faithfulness to their oath of office, diligence in meeting responsibilities, and kindness—all means of disseminating agape.

Because, as noted, many if not most secular venues prohibit overt ministry, infusing agape into them through the Fruit of the Spirit has become all the more important. Christians manifesting the Fruit of the Spirit throughout our society prevent it from deteriorating into a banana republic, instead promoting an environment characterized by integrity, decency, honesty, fidelity, and other virtues.

Jesus, in the Sermon on the Mount, commands us to function as salt, preserving our arena of existence from decay.

Integrity, kindness, and genuine concern for others are becoming scarce commodities in contemporary American society, making the contribution of believers in secular settings all the more valuable. Consequently, it is important that we produce significant quantities of agape by radiating the Fruit of the Spirit in our spheres of influence.

Those arenas often comprise venues where others cannot go, thus providing unique opportunities to spread agape. For example, Christians working in ambulances and operating rooms, courtrooms and prisons, large corporations and the news and entertainment industry, are uniquely situated to display agape through disseminating the Fruit of the Spirit, venues where it is desperately needed. Merely being the person God designed us to be represents a potent expression of agape that adds significant profit to our bottom line as CEO of Agape Inc.

Frequently we display the Fruit of the Spirit through what we might label as micro-expressions of agape, even though they can have a macro-sized impact. We can convey agape with our tone of voice, choice of words, attitude, body language, facial expression, and other aspects of our personalities.

Dr. Jerome Motto told the story of a man living in the San Francisco area who left his apartment one evening, walked to the Golden Gate Bridge, climbed over the four-foot guardrail, and plunged to his death in the waters 220 feet below. Dr. Motto reported,

> I went to this guy's apartment afterward with the assistant medical examiner... The guy was in his thirties, lived alone, pretty bare apartment. He'd written a note and left it on his bureau. It said, "I'm going to walk to the bridge. If one person smiles at me on the way, I will not jump."[iii]

We live in a society that is becoming increasingly devoid of these micro-expressions of agape. The good news is that we can have a transforming effect in a world transfixed on microaggressions by flooding it with micro-expressions of agape.

Doing Tasks for which God Designed Us

In addition to producing agape by being the person God designed us to be, we can also convey agape to others, benefit them, by developing and exercising the capabilities God has implanted in us, our unique blend of natural and spiritual gifts. I discuss these gifts in a future chapter, so I will wait until then to expand on this topic.

When discussing the employment of our gifts to produce agape, the minds of many evangelicals gravitate toward evangelism, pastoring, teaching a Bible study, or some other activity we traditionally categorize as "ministry." Though these do present potent means of producing agape, engagement in virtually every occupation holds the potential of producing agape, since agape refers to benefiting others, and most occupations can achieve that objective.

Let me put a sharper point on what I am saying. We might think of a medical doctor producing agape by having Christian literature in his or her waiting room or talking about the Lord in the course of helping people medically. Though those practices represent significant means of displaying agape, I am saying that the doctor predominantly displays agape by helping his patients get better—by stopping the sickness and pain and restoring them to health. Likewise, virtually every occupation has agape producing potential. The accountant benefits people by helping them keep their finances straight so that they can live responsibly. The electrician blesses people by providing homes in which all the electrical circuits function safely and well, bringing power to many appliances that benefit their lives. The checkout clerk at Walmart enables people to buy needed items. The stay-at-home mom enjoys one of the greatest venues for producing agape by caring for her children and influencing them to grow into godly, responsible, socially adjusted individuals. Her investment is multiplied as her children in turn mold future generations.

The Foundational Nature of Being the Person God Designed Us to Be

The potential of all professions to produce agape raises a significant question. Is every person in every profession producing agape just by virtue of doing their jobs? The apostle Paul answers that question in the opening verses of 1 Corinthians 13, the love chapter, by asserting:

> If I speak in the tongues of men and of angels, but have not love, I am a noisy gong or a clanging cymbal. And if I have prophetic powers, and understand all mysteries and all knowledge, and if I have all faith, so as to remove mountains, but have not love, I am nothing. If I give away all I have, and if I deliver up my body to be burned, but have not love, I gain nothing.

In this passage Paul conveys that a personality displaying agape provides the necessary foundation for actions that display agape. Agape orientated actions not undergirded by the Fruit of the Spirit are counterproductive. A selfish personality will warp every endeavor. Whatever our occupation, if we are grumpy, impatient, or dishonest, rather than blessing others through our work, we will be a thorn in their flesh. A grumpy, impatient nurse will ultimately have a negative impact on a patient, regardless of how good her nursing skills might be. The old adage applies, "People don't care how much we know until they know how much we care."

Happily, the converse is also true. As we approach our occupation with a personality that exudes agape toward employers, employees, coworkers, customers, patients, and clients, that display of agape will enhance their experience of our professional skills. Whatever our occupation, we can use it to display agape through the combined impact of our personality and professional skills.

Displaying Agape Directly and Indirectly

We can use our capabilities to produce agape directly or

indirectly. Building someone a good home or leading a Bible study provides direct benefit to them. Earning money so that we can support various ministries represents an indirect means of displaying agape. The person earning the money is often several layers removed from the person receiving its benefit. In many cases they will never meet here on earth. The impersonal nature of ministries such as earning money to help others may cause us to view them as less meaningful forms of agape production. A more thoughtful analysis, however, reveals that this is not the case. Churches could not function and missionaries could not stay on the field apart from the person working in the shop or office to support them.

The ministry of FARMS International helps needy Christians in Third World countries by providing them with interest-free loans, usually of several hundred dollars, that enable them to start a business that will lift them out of poverty and provide them with dignity, a decent standard of living, and the capacity to give. This arrangement includes the requirement to return the money loaned to them, which over 90% do. It is amazing to think that a gift of a few hundred dollars to this ministry can elevate the life of a Christian family living in squalor to economic stability and dignity. Money can comprise a significant tool for displaying agape.

Similar Fruit but Different Gifts

These two forms of agape, who we are and what we do, differ in that the Fruit of the Spirit is largely generic while natural and spiritual gifts are individual.

We do not have one list of the Fruit of the Spirit for one person and a different list for others. We are all seeking to produce the same fruit. And while the various manifestations of the Fruit of the Spirit may look slightly different when displayed by different personalities, they nonetheless possess essentially the same characteristics.

By way of contrast, the Gifts of the Spirit are diverse. Scripture makes a point of that. In 1 Corinthians 12:4-6 Paul observes,

> Now there are varieties of gifts, but the same Spirit; and there are varieties of service, but the same Lord; and there are varieties of activities, but it is the same God who empowers them all in everyone.

Our natural gifts also reflect this diversity. Some individuals are great at math, some at speaking, and others at athletics. Therefore, our production of agape through natural and spiritual gifts is unique. One person may display agape through teaching while another does so through helps or administration.

Therefore, agape displays a sameness for all believers in the Fruit of the Spirit while it manifests uniqueness through the Gifts of the Spirit.

By our physical birth we have characteristics common to all human beings that identify us as human. We have similar body parts, temperature, etc. We also have differences that identify us as individuals, especially in our capabilities. The same is true of our spiritual birth. The Fruit of the Spirit by providing us with a godly personality identifies us as belonging to the family of God, yet we display individuality through our unique package of the Gifts of the Spirit.

Preparation for Agape Production

Virtually all agape production requires some sort of groundwork—some foundational preparation. A tradesman needs to learn his trade and a doctor goes through many phases of training. Maintaining spiritual vitality requires adequate time in Bible study and prayer. Pastors need to do sermon preparation and Bible study leaders are required to prepare their material. Even giving requires that we do research to ensure that we are using our financial resources most effectively.

Consequently, preparation represents a major component of producing agape. It may not be viewed as an expression of agape per se since it does not directly benefit others, that is, during the preparation phase no one is helped directly.

These preparations, however, provide the foundation for benefiting others later, and therefore they should be viewed as expressions of agape. This is important to recognize since during the preparation stage we may feel that we are not being productive, and we might neglect adequate preparation for that reason. That, of course, is a shortsighted perspective.

We have been considering that the Lord designed and commissioned us as CEO of our lives to produce agape. Just how interested is He in our maximizing agape output? The next chapter addresses that question.

Principle #4
Pursue Maximum Profit

In hiring Joe, the board assigned him the specific task of maximizing profit. They had each invested a substantial amount of money in the ABC Widget Company, and they charged Joe with earning the greatest possible return for them. Joe had done enough research on these investors/board members to know that they were all sufficiently well-off financially that they did not actually need the profit, but he also knew that each of them had achieved financial success by pursuing maximum profit in everything they did, and their investment in ABC Widget Company was no exception.

They expected Joe to operate within certain parameters in

producing that return. Though aggressive businessmen, they also possessed a high level of integrity. They had not achieved their long-term success by dishonesty or cutting corners but rather by wise investments and maintaining a reputation for integrity. They had hired Joe because their research indicated that he was also a person of integrity. Consequently, they did not want Joe to sabotage competitors, misrepresent the company's product, underpay employees, etc. However, within those ethical and practical confines, they wanted Joe to aggressively and creatively pursue the maximum amount of profit possible.

God's Definition of Success

In previous chapters we concluded that agape production comprises our purpose for existence. Consequently, God's definition of success for our lives consists not only of producing agape but of maximizing its production. As CEO of Agape Inc., the more profit I make with the resources God has given me, the more successful I am.

Regarding maximum output, the apostle Paul gave this charge:

> Do you not know that in a race all the runners run, but only one receives the prize? So run that you may obtain it. Every athlete exercises self-control in all things. They do it to receive a perishable wreath, but we an imperishable. (1 Corinthians 9:24-25)

No one ever won a boxing match or race by maintaining a comfortable, average effort or speed. Rather, winning demands total focus, discipline, and effort that takes us out of our comfort zone. In the verses that follow, Paul describes the discipline essential for success:

> So I do not run aimlessly; I do not box as one beating the air. But I discipline my body and keep it under control, lest after preaching to others I myself should be disqualified. (1 Corinthians 9:26-27)

Jerry Rice, who played as a wide receiver for the San Francisco 49ers and has been inducted into the Pro-football Hall of Fame, holds virtually every significant career receiving record, including most receptions (1,549), receiving yards (22,895), all-purpose yards (23,546), touchdown receptions (197), and consecutive games with at least one catch (274).[iv] He described his work ethic by asserting, "Today I will do what others won't, so tomorrow I can do what others can't."[v]

He described the reason for his success by reflecting,

> I don't think I'm such a natural, I think what I'm doing is very hard work. I work hard to keep in shape, I work hard on the practice field, I work hard in a game. Cornerbacks are the best athletes on the team; they wouldn't be out there if they weren't. Those are the guys I have to beat. It isn't easy."[vi]

His commitment to go above and beyond paid off on the football field.

The apostle Paul expressed a similar total commitment, his to agape production, as follows:

> We put no obstacle in anyone's way, so that no fault may be found with our ministry, but as servants of God we commend ourselves in every way: by great endurance, in afflictions, hardships, calamities, beatings, imprisonments, riots, labors, sleepless nights, hunger; by purity, knowledge, patience, kindness, the Holy Spirit, genuine love; by truthful speech, and the power of God; with the weapons of righteousness for the right hand and for the left.... (2 Corinthians 6:3-7)

In other words, Paul would suffer any hardship and pursue any objective that would enhance his agape output. He would not settle for any outcome other than maximum agape production. He was committed to winning the race.

Pursuit of Maximum Profit

We understand God's interest in our maximizing profit when we reflect on how much He has invested in this enterprise. God the Father designed it. God the Son gave His life on the cross to buy the company and provide its working capital. God the Holy Spirit is working in the life of every believer day and night to provide direction and power. In light of this considerable investment, it is reasonable that God desires maximum profit.

Numerous passages of Scripture convey God's interest in profit. The apostle Paul speaks of this focus on maximum profit in 1 Corinthians 6:12: "All things are lawful for me, but not all things are profitable. All things are lawful for me, but I will not be mastered by anything." (NASB) In essence he is saying that he does not make decisions based on legality but profitability. We might debate over whether I have a right to take a second piece of pie for dessert. Paul would tell me to forget about whether I have a right to consume it but instead challenge me to make the decision based on whether it is profitable to consume it. Does that second piece of pie benefit anyone or is it a liability to agape production?

He advances a similar line of reasoning in 1 Corinthians 10:23: "All things are lawful, but not all things are profitable. All things are lawful, but not all things edify." (NASB) Here he contends that our criterion for making decisions should be edification, that is, to build up others. This is clearly a reference to agape, of benefitting another person.

Perhaps the most direct scriptural teaching related to maximizing profit resides in the parables of the talents (Matthew 25:14-30) and minas (Luke 19:12-26). Though similar in many ways, a closer examination reveals that these parables embody a significant distinction.

Both speak of a master preparing to go on a long journey, apparently a reference to the ascension of Jesus to heaven after His resurrection and the church age to follow. In both parables this master provides a substantial amount of money to his servants, expecting them to use it most profitably. When he returns, he calls these servants to give an account.

The two parables differ in that in the parable of the talents the master gives different numbers of talents to each servant whereas the parable of the minas has him giving each the same—one mina.

Giving differing numbers of talents seems to convey that the Lord has distributed different quantities of gifts to His people. The parable records that the person receiving five talents earned five more and the one receiving two talents earned two more. Apparently the parable is teaching that both maximized profit commensurate with what they received. As a result, the parable records that both of these received exactly the same reward. Note that the response of the master to both of these servants is exactly the same.

> Now after a long time the master of those servants came and settled accounts with them. And he who had received the five talents came forward, bringing five talents more, saying, 'Master, you delivered to me five talents; here, I have made five talents more.' His master said to him, 'Well done, good and faithful servant. You have been faithful over a little; I will set you over much. Enter into the joy of your master.' And he also who had the two talents came forward, saying, 'Master, you delivered to me two talents; here, I have made two talents more.' His master said to him, 'Well done, good and faithful servant. You have been faithful over a little; I will set you over much. Enter into the joy of your master.' (Matthew 25:19-23)

This parable provides comfort in assuring us that our success as CEO of our lives is not determined by the number of talents we have received and the related amount of profit we make but by our faithfulness in investing what we have been given to the fullest. We can rejoice that God blessed Billy Graham with tremendous gifts, but we do not need to feel inferior because we have fewer gifts or because we have produced less fruit.

By way of contrast, the parable of the minas has each one

receiving one mina. This seems to convey that God has given each of us one life and holds us responsible for its optimal investment. With his one mina, one servant earned 10 minas and another servant earned five. Since both started out with one, this seems to convey that one of these two servants worked twice as hard as the other. He was more diligent, more creative, and more aggressive in pursuing profit.

This parable has these two servants receiving differing responses from the master, both in regard to commendation and reward.

> When he returned, having received the kingdom, he ordered these servants to whom he had given the money to be called to him, that he might know what they had gained by doing business. The first came before him, saying, 'Lord, your mina has made ten minas more.' And he said to him, 'Well done, good servant! Because you have been faithful in a very little, you shall have authority over ten cities.' And the second came, saying, 'Lord, your mina has made five minas.' And he said to him, 'And you are to be over five cities.' (Luke 19:15-19)

The more diligent servant received 10 cities while the other one received only five. The master commended the more diligent servant by saying, "Well done, good servant! Because you have been faithful in a very little, you shall have authority over ten cities." To the servant who earned five, he merely said, "And you are to be over five cities." Therefore, in this parable, the servant earning more received both a commendation and 10 cities whereas the one earning less received no commendation and only five cities.

Both of these parables record a third servant who produces nothing.

In the parable of the minas, the amount earned seems to reflect the level of commitment and hard work displayed by the recipients. The parable seems to be conveying that all of the servants had the potential to earn 10 minas, but of the three that the master evaluates in the parable, only one fully utilized that potential. He is fully rewarded for his efforts.

The three respondents in the parable of the minas might be portrayed in terms of three 18-wheeler drivers, each assigned a similar truck by his employer straight from the factory. He instructs them to get their trucks loaded at the dock in New York and haul the load to St. Louis, a distance of 950 miles, where the goods will be unloaded and placed in a warehouse for distribution. Each trip makes more profit for the owner. In effect, each driver possesses the same capability for production.

One driver, however, wanting to produce the maximum for the owner, aggressively pursues creative ways to make more profit. He talks the dockworkers in New York into allowing him to help load, which enables him to start his trip to St. Louis several hours earlier. He discovers that legally he can drive two extra hours per day, getting him to St. Louis even sooner. He drives six days per week instead of five. By studying maps and traffic patterns, he finds an alternate route that allows him to complete the trip an hour faster. This driver also helps with the unloading process at St. Louis, reducing the overall time by another couple of hours. These initiatives enable him to make an extra half trip each week or two extra trips per month. His most productive effort, though, resides in his hunting down a St. Louis company needing product shipped to New York. Therefore, instead of deadheading it back to the New York dock, he returns with a full load, virtually doubling the owner's profits in addition to the extra two trips per month.

A second driver follows the standard, prescribed approach, getting his truck loaded in New York and unloaded in St. Louis, putting in an honest day's work, five days per week. This enables him to make one round-trip per week, including the time required for loading and unloading. In so doing he makes a good profit for the owner but does not go above and beyond as did the first driver. He had the capability to earn the same profit as the first driver, but he did not take the initiative, preferring a comfortable approach.

The third driver, being very lazy, just sits in his truck at the dock in New York. He turns on the truck in order to run the heater or air conditioner for his comfort and to charge his cell phone. He spends all day every day doing FaceTime with several girlfriends and listening to music, but he never hauls anything. However, his presence in the truck does serve the purpose of preventing it from being damaged or stolen. Since the owner has a good-sized fleet, this indolent driver is confident that the owner will never check up on him.

During an annual analysis of his drivers' performances, the owner of the truck fleet commends the first driver who used his initiative and worked hard, and rewards him with a substantial bonus, a parallel to the servant in the parable of the minas receiving an enthusiastic commendation and 10 cities.

As with the servant who earned five minas, the owner of the truck fleet, though satisfied with a driver who ran his route faithfully every week, does not express the same enthusiasm for him that he did for the one showing substantially more initiative and working much harder. And though the owner gives this second driver a bonus, it is not as large as that awarded to the driver who worked much harder.

Needless to say, the owner does catch up with the third driver and demands that he account for his actions. The best defense this lazy driver can think of is that by sitting in the truck all day, he kept it safe from those who would damage or steal it. So he proudly says to the owner, "Here is your truck in almost mint condition." The owner is not impressed.

The parable in which each person received one mina seems to convey that whatever your gift package might be, if you are creative, aggressive, and hard-working, you possess the capacity to make a tenfold profit. You may opt for being a faithful plodder that does a responsible job but no more. You are willing to work at a comfortable pace for the Lord but not push beyond your comfort zone. You are reliable in making your one trip per week, but no more. You could earn 10 minas but are willing to settle for five. Our analysis above suggests that this level of work results in reward but not optimal success. This level of achievement does not represent succeeding as CEO of our lives nor what the Lord advocates in Scripture. Rather, winning the race requires maximum effort—pursuing a ten mina result.

The bottom line is this: success is not determined by the size or nature of our package of gifts (the number of talents we have received) but has everything to do with our commitment and effort in using our package of gifts (mina) to earn maximum profit. For some readers the comfortable, five mina approach might have appeal. They may conclude, "I will give a comfortable amount of money, serve a comfortable amount of time, and display a "reasonable" amount of agape in relationships, and that way I can live comfortably here on earth and do okay in heaven also.

However, as we noted, a mediocre performance results only in a mediocre reward. This may not concern some believers because heaven seems to be far away, in the distant future, and somewhat surreal. Therefore, from their current perspective heavenly rewards do not seem all that important. However, when the time comes we will realize the overwhelming importance of the Lord's commendation and the eternal reward granted to a 10 mina person.

The person settling for a 5 mina performance might respond, "Well, Jesus included the five mina person in the parable, and conveys that he receives a reward. Therefore, being one of those people must be okay." Notice that the parable never advocates being a five mina person but only indicates that some will take this approach to life.

The apostle Paul challenges us to run the race so as to win. Succeeding as CEO of our lives requires the diligence, drive, and determination to produce at the 10 mina level for the Lord.

This chapter has stressed the need for us to maximize agape production in order to succeed as CEO of our lives. Doing so requires that we make optimal decisions. The chapter ahead explains how we can do that.

Principle #5
Access Guidance
from the Holy Spirit

Joe's position as a new CEO confronted him with many significant decisions. He had to decide how much time to devote to work and how much to spend with the family. He knew that the demands of the new job would require more than usual time at the office, but he wanted to be sensitive to his family's needs also. He had to determine the best tone to establish with employees, whether he should be all business, friendly, or some combination of the two. He had to decide who he could trust and how much. A decision was necessary on how to structure the debt left by the previous CEO and how to deal with immediate challenges to the operation. He needed to decide how to schedule his days so that he was investing his time where it was needed most.

The list of decisions confronting him seemed to be endless. Some were especially crucial because they would establish the tone for his administration. Mistakes could have long-term, serious implications. These decisions were complicated by the fact that each one affected other aspects of the operation. Spending more time studying the company's finances left less time to focus on production issues.

Though CEO, he nonetheless felt that these challenges were above his pay grade. Because Joe was a believer, he understood and engaged in the process for receiving guidance from the Holy Spirit, and he employed that process in making these decisions. The months that followed revealed the wisdom supplied by the Holy Spirit's guidance.

Our Partnership with the Holy Spirit

The Lord commissioned us to function as CEO of our lives, but knowing our limitations He assigned the Holy Spirit as a partner in this enterprise. He is especially helpful in the decision-making process.

A major factor in making a partnership work consists of clearly defining the role of each partner and then functioning within that framework. Consequently, our partnership with the Holy Spirit can only function effectively if we develop a concise understanding of His role and ours.

The Holy Spirit Does not Replace Us as CEO

Since God assigned the Holy Spirit as our partner, it seems surprising that we would retain the role of CEO of our life. It would seem that the Holy Spirit should assume that position. That, however, is not God's design. Scripture refers to the Holy Spirit as a helper, and He serves in that capacity in our partnership.

The functioning of the Holy Spirit as our partner is graphically described by the apostle Paul in Romans 8:26 where he informs us that "the Spirit helps us in our weakness." The very descriptive Greek word for "helps" here means "to take hold together with someone." One person is seeking to achieve a task too difficult for him, and a friend helps by grabbing hold along with him. This word describes the nature of the Holy Spirit's partnership with us.

This term brings John to mind, a man who just started his own business and has at his home a heavy machine that he needs to load on his pickup truck and take to his new shop. He is able to use a hand truck to get the machine out to his driveway where his pickup is parked. He lowers the tailgate and tries to lift the machine onto the truck. He manages to get it off the ground and lifts it up to within a few inches of the level of the truck bed but just can't get it up high enough. On the second try he is getting tired and misses by about a foot. The third attempt just barely gets it off the ground.

Just when he is about to despair, he hears a voice behind him. "Hey buddy, need a hand." It is his neighbor, Bill, a tall, broad-shouldered guy in his mid-thirties. John, looking encouraged responds, "I sure do." Bill grabs hold of the opposite side of the machine and together they lift it into the truck without a problem. In fact, it felt like Bill was shouldering most of the load.

John thanked Bill but then started to wonder how he was going to unload the machine at the shop. In seeking to achieve that, gravity would be on his side but may give him too much help. He could envision dropping the machine and it crashing to the ground in pieces. Just then he noticed that Bill was opening the passenger door of his truck, and he heard him say, "I suspect you will need some help getting that unloaded. Let's roll. I got you covered."

That scenario depicts our partnership with the Holy Spirit. He leaves us in charge of the operation, fully engaged, and responsible for pursuing the related objectives, but He is there to provide help as we need it, especially in supplying guidance and power.

Our specific concern in this chapter is determining how the Holy Spirit provides guidance. If the Holy Spirit took over our role as CEO, we would no longer have the responsibility to make decisions. He would assume that responsibility. However, since in God's design we maintain the role of CEO, we retain the responsibility for decision making. Yet, since our partner, the Holy Spirit, has infinite wisdom, we would be wise to glean guidance from Him. The question confronting us in this chapter is how do we access that guidance?

The Holy Spirit Does not Want to Control Us

In determining how we derive guidance from the Holy Spirit, we must first recognize that the Holy Spirit does not guide us by controlling us. Just turning over control of our lives to the Holy Spirit would resolve the guidance issue. If He controlled us, robot-like we would be passive in the process, merely responding as He worked the controls. However, this arrangement is not compatible with God's design. Instead, God assigns us control over our lives to make and implement decisions regarding the utilization of our time, money, and other resources.

The misconception that the Holy Spirit wants to control our lives probably stems from the misinterpretation of passages such as Ephesians 5:18. You have probably heard speakers assert that when Paul instructs, "(B)e filled with the Spirit," he really means that we should be controlled by the Spirit. However, the passage does not say that, and the Holy Spirit does not want to control us. Satan wants to control us and in fact does control many people through drugs, alcohol, lust, greed, pride, etc. By way of contrast, the Holy Spirit is not in the control business but instead wants us to control our lives, utilizing His guidance and power, to achieve His purposes.

Other evangelical concepts also promote the error that the Holy Spirit wants to take control of our lives. For example, the old cliché, "Let go and let God," conveys that living the Christian life entails taking our hands off the controls and letting God take over. This arrangement also leaves us passive in the process of living the Christian life—robots being controlled by God to achieve His purposes. We need not make any decisions.

Some days—in fact many days—I would just love to turn over the control of my life to the Holy Spirit and let him take it from here. That would be a whole while easier, but that is not God's plan.

Had God wanted robots for followers, He easily could have created them, and they would have given Him a lot less grief than have human beings. However, just as you probably would not prefer a robot for a spouse, at least not most of the time, God prefers human beings for His children and followers. Consequently, He calls us to function humanly by maintaining control of our lives and employing our minds and wills in order to advance His agenda.

If Christian living consisted of turning the control of our life over to the Holy Spirit, the content of the New Testament would be entirely different. Instead of containing many commands, it would just keep repeating the same command, "Turn your life over to the control of the Holy Spirit, and you will spontaneously live as I want you to live." Instead of instructing, "Abstain from every form of evil," (1 Thessalonians 5:22) the passage would merely state, "Turn your life over to the control of the Holy Spirit and you will instinctively abstain from every form of evil." The point is that the whole flow of Scripture conveys that God wants us to maintain control of our lives and achieve His purposes through managing them.

Let's reflect on this truth using an analogy. Someone came up with the bumper sticker, "God is my copilot." Soon others began to object, indicating that God needs to be the pilot, and we should place ourselves in the copilot's seat. A more biblical perspective is that God owns the airline and has hired us to be pilots. Because of the limitations of our knowledge and skills, the Lord knew that we would crash a lot of airplanes, so He assigned the Holy Spirit to be our co-pilot. In doing so, He has not relieved us of our piloting responsibilities. We still must study the principles in the Word for successfully piloting our lives, analyze what flight plan will lead to the optimal agape production, and exercise the necessary disciplines to fly the plane proficiently.

Though making the case that God does not want to control us may sound like an insignificant technical distinction, it is not. I have heard believers assert, "I tried to live the Christian life but kept failing. Then I realized my mistake. I was trying to do it instead of letting the Holy Spirit do it. I decided to turn control of my life over to Him, and since then I have experienced success in my Christian walk."

This perspective on Christian living has always intrigued me for two reasons. First, I do not find this arrangement with the Holy Spirit in Scripture. In addition, in my experience the Christian life requires work, discipline, and struggle against a full array of temptations such as eating too much and speaking when I should be listening. I wanted to discover how these individuals just let the Holy Spirit do it, which seemed to be much easier than my approach to the Christian life. However, I never could get them to explain how that worked. How do I get the Holy Spirit to take control? I also wondered how it worked for them in the long run. As I watched their lives I noticed that after a while they tended to crash and burn. I concluded that the secret they thought they had discovered comprises an unbiblical approach to the Christian life that does not work. The Holy Spirit has not bought into this arrangement.

In management circles, the attempt by an employee to get his supervisor to assume his responsibilities is referred to as "delegating up." Seeking to assign the Holy Spirit our responsibilities as CEO of our lives by putting Him in control entails delegating up. This approach does not work in the corporate world. Will Brewer, President of Performance-Solutions-Group, Inc. observes, "(D)elegating up, in all but a few instances, helps neither party and is counterproductive."[vii] Delegating up produces similar results in the spiritual realm.

If we managed to delegate up and turn the responsibilities of flying the plane over to the Holy Spirit, that would reduce our role to passenger, since the Holy Spirit does not need our help as co-pilot. That would be a very comfortable arrangement, alleviating us of the responsibilities of flying the plane and instead leaving us with the luxury of relaxing in first class while the flight attendant served us coke and peanuts. This arrangement might have substantial appeal, except that it is not biblical nor does it work in the real world.

We cannot delegate the responsibility for managing our lives to anyone else, not even the Holy Spirit. We must live in the awareness that God has left us in control of our hands, feet, mouth, and a full array of resources and holds us responsible to use them effectively.

How Does the Holy Spirit Communicate Direction to Us?

Since the Holy Spirit does not desire to control us, He must convey His guidance to us in some way. But how?

Imagine you are a guest on one of those HGTV programs. You have looked at four houses, and now you must decide whether you will buy the ranch-style out in the country with 3 acres for $425,000, the two-story brick home in the suburbs for $450,000, a larger brand-new home in a new development for $475,000, or the spacious, upscale townhouse closer to your work for $465,000.

In deciding, you must process a huge number of factors: the price, square footage, floor plan, cost of needed renovations, time and cost of commuting, the kid's schools, taxes, landscaping (the house in the new development has minimal landscaping), age of the house, the neighborhood, type of HVAC, aesthetics, and many other factors. Consequently, you are keenly aware of your need for the Holy Spirit to guide you. The question is, how will He communicate that guidance?

One obvious answer resides in guidance from Scripture. For example, we must consider any ethical issues related to these choices. Rumors around town indicate that the single man occupying the other half of the townhouse is living an openly promiscuous life and selling drugs. The police have not been able to catch him, but the rumors, nonetheless, seem to be reliable. A biblical view of life would militate against exposing your family to this type of environment. This concern reduces your options to three.

However, no explicit mandates from Scripture are available

to help you to decide among the remaining three houses. How will Holy Spirit communicate which of these is the optimal choice? Let me suggest five of the most popular perspectives.

Options

One means of guidance used by the Holy Spirit in Scripture is direct communication. Verses come to mind such as Acts 8:29, "And the Spirit said to Philip, 'Go over and join this chariot.'" The Lord might somehow audibly speak to you as He did to Philip. As you drive up to the two-story brick house you hear a voice saying, "This is the one." Only you and your spouse are in the car, and that voice sounded nothing like your spouse's.

A second approach, employed by many people, entails seeking and believing that God will give them a sign. We see this approach to guidance in the story of Gideon and the fleece. In seeking to determine which house is God's best, you may pray for some sort of sign. Then as you walk through the ranch-style house you see a cross hanging on the otherwise bare walls, perhaps left by the previous occupants. You conclude that this constitutes God's indication that this is the house.

Many Christians look to the Holy Spirit to guide through a third means, that of providing us with a subjective experience as an indicator of His leading. "Every time I go into that two-story brick house, I feel a deep peace. I believe that God is telling me that this is His choice."

A fourth, perspective on guidance resides in the belief of some Christians that barring any explicit biblical directives related to the available options, God has given us the freedom to choose for ourselves. There is no particular house that reflects "His will," and therefore we are free to choose whichever we like the most and think would be a wise selection. In other words, within the boundaries set by the direct teachings of Scripture, we should not expect any guidance from the Holy Spirit.

A fifth alternative consists of the Holy Spirit guiding our thought process as we apply the related *principles* of Scripture to the situation confronting us, especially the principles related to maximizing agape production and how we can achieve that. This alternative requires that we thoroughly familiarize ourselves with the principles of Scripture related to our current decision, gather information on the available options, and then apply those biblical principles to the options under consideration, with special focus on which choice lends itself to maximum agape production. As we do our part, the Holy Spirit guides our thought processes toward the best choice.

This approach differs from the previous one in that it not only considers the explicit directives of Scripture but also scriptural principles. Those principles provide us with far more extensive guidance than the mere mandates of Scripture. It differs from the earlier option mentioned related to some sort of experiential guidance in that this approach views the Holy Spirit as working through our minds as opposed to our emotions.

Analysis

It would seem optimal if the Holy Spirit used option #1 all of the time, directly communicating guidance to us. Though He might audibly tell you to buy the two-story brick home, the odds are slim that He will. It seems that this is not the Lord's usual way of conveying His directions to us. In fact, this was far from the norm even in biblical times.

We make hundreds, if not thousands of choices every day, and it is not reasonable or scriptural to assume that the Holy Spirit will be providing direct communication for most of those decisions. "Lord, should I pack lunch or go out to eat?" "Today you should pack a pastrami and Swiss on rye and a kosher dill." If a person does receive direct communication, it will probably only occur several times during his lifetime. For the overwhelming majority of our decisions, the Holy Spirit will guide in some other form.

We run into the same problem with signs. It is possible that the Holy Spirit may provide some sort of sign as we seek to make a major decision in life, but we have few examples of this approach to guidance in Scripture and little indication that it represents God's norm—that the Holy Spirit will provide a sign leading us to pack a lunch. "Just as I went to pack my lunch the cooking show was featuring a pastrami and Swiss sandwich. Maybe that was a sign from God."

This approach also confronts us with the problem of knowing whether phenomena we believe to be signs from God actually are. Was the cross on the wall of the ranch house really a sign from God? Maybe. However, you may have conveyed to the realtor that you are a Christian, and perhaps he put it up to prompt you to purchase that house.

We have no biblical basis for believing that God provides signs for all or even most of our choices. Assuming that He does could stress us out as we try to find signs for everything and determine if they actually are signs from God. Gideon specifically stipulated the terms of the sign, which included a supernatural dimension, giving assurance that its fulfillment was the work of God. The cross on the wall carries with it no such assurance. A parallel to Gideon's approach would call us to pray specifically that we would find a cross on the wall and *then* discover it. Most Christians who seek guidance from signs do not employ this Gideon-type approach that requires evidence of supernatural involvement. If most of the time God is not leading through signs, our looking for and depending on them could result in a lot of bad choices.

The same might be said for experiential urgings. Many Christians lean toward this indicator as a major means of communication from the Holy Spirit. Perhaps this inclination stems from teaching on Proverbs 3:5-6, especially in light of the King James translation of this passage. I provide the New King James here. "Trust in the LORD with all your heart, And lean not on your own understanding; In all your ways acknowledge Him, And He shall direct your paths." It has often been taught that in this passage Solomon is instructing us not to follow the directions of our "carnal reasoning" but rather to follow the promptings we sense in our heart, i.e. feelings, which are viewed as being the ministry of the Holy Spirit.

Several problems exist with this perspective. First, though

the passage might be construed to be referring to a subjective experience, it does not say that. Solomon did not write, "In all your ways acknowledge your feelings," but instead He said, "In all your ways acknowledge Him." Does acknowledging God refer to following our feelings—internal urgings? The context suggests otherwise. It indicates that Solomon's prohibition against leaning to "your own understanding," is warning against following the mind uninformed by Scripture and instead to formulate decisions based on the teachings of Scripture.

For example, several verses later he instructs, "Honor the LORD with your wealth and with the firstfruits of all your produce." (Proverbs 3:9) A mind uninformed by Scripture, our own understanding, may lead us to believe that happiness results from using all our money for ourselves. One can easily see how a person whose thinking is not guided by Scripture would come to that conclusion. Instead, a mind informed by Scripture instructs us that all our resources belong to God and therefore we should be guided by the principles of Scripture in their use. Scripture also tells us that we derive more joy from giving than from keeping our resources for our own pleasure.

A major problem with guiding our lives by subjective experiences is that God's basic design for the human being calls us to employ our minds and not our feelings to guide our lives. On the human plane, we make good decisions by using our minds, by rational analysis of alternatives. You love the house in the new development, but the crack running down the wall suggests problems with the foundation, making it an irrational choice, despite assurances from the realtor. By way of contrast, feelings comprise the worst GPS for our lives. Our feelings tend to tell us to eat too much, spend too much, and work too little. God designed our minds and not our feeling as the primary means of guiding our lives.

Likewise, on the spiritual plane, God has communicated to us through His Word, which requires the employment of our minds to understand and apply. The view that the Holy Spirit does not work through our mental processes, but instead works primarily through our emotions, finds no scriptural support. It seems improbable that the Holy Spirit would cast aside God's basic design for human guidance and the instructions of the Word to guide us primarily through subjective nudgings, especially since Scripture encourages the employment of our minds in discerning God's will and since our emotions represent the instrument most likely to guide us in the wrong direction.

This feelings perspective on the Holy Spirit's direction also confronts us with the same problem we encountered with signs. We make many decisions within the course of the day. Should we expect emotional urgings for each one? And if the urgings we feel are not from the Holy Spirit, we face the prospect of making bad decisions. Related to this is the anxiety resulting from constantly trying to discern whether promptings are from the Holy Spirit and what they are telling us. Doing so can create apprehension and confusion. Did I experience those warm feelings when the realtor took me through the two-story brick house because God was telling me that it was His choice or because it reminded me of the house where I grew up?

As already mentioned, the fifth alternative differs from the fourth in that it not only considers the explicit commands of Scripture but also the *principles* of Scripture. The explicit commands of Scripture may reduce the number of house choices from 4 to 3, but the principles of Scripture provide substantially more input, especially as we consider the comprehensive scriptural teaching to optimize agape output.

The application of scriptural principles in determining which house to purchase, especially the principle of maximizing agape, prompts numerous questions. Does one house better care for the needs of our family—an important expression of agape? Is one safer? Time embodies an important resource for producing agape. Does one make better use of our time in terms of the distance of the commute or time required for upkeep (mowing three acres)? Will one home better lend itself to ministry—accommodating a Bible study? Does one option enhance relaxation and recreation, which in turn will enable us to serve others more effectively?

Pondering the choice from an agape perspective leads us to consider that if we can save $25,000 on a home without losing any other advantages, we can use that money to benefit others. If we can cut our commute 30 minutes each way, that gives us an extra hour each day, five hours per week, about 250 hours a year—equivalent to over six work weeks, to minister to our family, neighbors, those in our church, or others. In addition, saving 15 miles each way, or 30 miles daily, at 50 cents a mile adds up to $15 per day or $75 per week, or $3750 per year. We could invest those funds in benefiting others in many ways, such as lifting many Christian families in Third World countries out of poverty. As we prayerfully make this analysis, the Holy Spirit guides our thought processes to enable us to identify the choice that will most significantly enhance our agape production.

Various passages of Scripture indicate that God expects us to use our minds in order to make decisions related to the management of our lives and that the Holy Spirit works through that process to guide our choices. For example, the apostle Paul says in Philippians 1:9-10:

> And it is my prayer that your love may abound more and more, with knowledge and all discernment, so that you may approve what is excellent, and so be pure and blameless for the day of Christ.

If the Holy Spirit predominantly guided us in the production of agape, "that your love may abound more and more," through signs or experiential promptings, we would not need "knowledge and all discernment." We would only need to wait for the Holy Spirit to provide the sign or urging in order to determine which options are "excellent." This verse, however, calls us to employ our minds.

The writer of Hebrews asserts:

> (F)or everyone who lives on milk is unskilled in the word of righteousness, since he is a child. But solid food is for the mature, for those who have their powers of discernment trained by constant practice to distinguish good from evil. (Hebrews 5:13-14)

Notice that this passage indicates that we should be led through the "word of righteousness," connoting that the principles of Scripture should be foundational to the guidance process. The word "discernment" in this passage is a judicial term, suggesting that we function like a judge who is exercising his mental capacities to analyze the case presented to him. If the Holy Spirit led predominantly through signs or subjective urgings, we would not need to develop our discernment through the practice of applying Scripture to the situations of life. We could make perfect decisions in every situation merely by following the signs or urgings supplied by the Holy Spirit. Instead, this passage suggests that we need to enhance our skill in decision-making, a capacity developed through the training of our minds to understand the principles of Scripture and to apply those principles to situations confronting us.

The apostle Paul also supports the position that the Holy Spirit works through our minds in passages such as Colossians 1:9-10:

> And so, from the day we heard, we have not ceased to pray for you, asking that you may be filled with the knowledge of his will in all spiritual wisdom and understanding, so as to walk in a manner worthy of the Lord, fully pleasing to him: bearing fruit in every good work and increasing in the knowledge of God.

In this passage Paul teaches that we should manage our lives in order to "walk in a manner worthy of the Lord" and bear "fruit in every good work." He indicates that we achieve this through "knowledge" and "all spiritual wisdom and understanding," that is, by means of the Holy Spirit enabling our minds to understand and apply spiritual principles.

We find the apostle Paul making a similar assertion in Romans 12:2, "Do not be conformed to this world, but be transformed by the renewal of your mind, that by testing you may discern what is the will of God, what is good and acceptable and perfect." This passage indicates that we do not discover "what is the will of God, what is good and acceptable and perfect," by seeking signs or sensing promptings, but by renewing our minds.

These and other passages all support the perspective that the Holy Spirit guides us predominantly through illuminating our minds so that we can apply the principles of Scripture in order to make optimal management decisions regarding agape production. We can be assured that the Holy Spirit will guide our minds to determine which of the houses under consideration is the best choice.

The Holy Spirit's Guidance through our Mind and the New Covenant

The unique partnership of believers with the Holy Spirit during the church age commenced with the institution of the New Covenant on the day of Pentecost. Under the Old Covenant, God placed His people under the authority of the Mosaic Law. As such, they functioned like menial slaves rather than executive level stewards. Without the unique partnership with the Holy Spirit provided by the New Covenant, they needed the explicit instructions on every aspect of life down to specific details contained in the Law.

In Galatians 4, the apostle Paul in describing life under the Old Covenant indicates that God dealt with His people as unskilled laborers and children.

> I mean that the heir, as long as he is a child, is no different from a slave, though he is the owner of everything, but he is under guardians and managers until the date set by his father. In the same way we also, when we were children, were enslaved to the elementary principles of the world. (Galatians 4:1-3)

Because a child lacks the capability to make consequential decisions, he is not given the freedom to do so, but instead he receives explicit guidance from parents, teachers, and others. What thinking parent would head for bed and say to his five-year-old, "Don't stay up too late." Instead, parents specifically tell five-year-olds when it is bedtime. Likewise, supervisors give unskilled servants specific instructions regarding what tasks to perform and how to perform them. This describes the believer's relationship with the Lord under the Old Covenant.

In the verses that follow the passage above, Paul describes the great transition from menial slave to executive in the family business that resulted from our adoption into the family of God under the New Covenant, and our corresponding new partnership with the Holy Spirit that enables us to function at that level.

> But when the fullness of time had come, God sent forth his Son, born of woman, born under the law, to redeem those who were under the law, so that we might receive adoption as sons. And because you are sons, God has sent the Spirit of his Son into our hearts, crying, "Abba! Father!" So you are no longer a slave, but a son, and if a son, then an heir through God. (Galatians 4:4-7)

In our culture we tend to think of adoption in terms of a married couple bringing home an infant or young child. That is not the idea here. Paul is portraying adoption from the Roman perspective, which suggests the picture of a successful businessman who has no heir adopting a capable young adult who under Roman law would be granted all the prerogatives of an executive in the family business. This would include authority to utilize all the family resources to produce maximum profit for the father who adopted him.

This was the case with the adoption of Augustus by Julius Caesar. In fact, his adoption did not occur while Julius Caesar was alive but instead was included in his will. Julius Caesar was murdered when Augustus was only 18 years old. Augustus nonetheless received authority over the estate of Julius and assumed his political position.

The Greek word for adoption literally means "to place as a son." Greek scholar M.R. Vincent describes the far-reaching implications of Roman adoption as follows:

> The process of legal adoption by which the chosen heir became entitled not only to the reversion of the property but to the civil status, to the burdens as well as the rights of the adopter - became, as it were, his other self, one with him....[viii]

In light of these implications of Roman adoption, *The Bible Knowledge Commentary* expresses the role of the believer resulting from his adoption by God as follows:

> All the enjoyments and privileges of a mature son in a family belong to those who have entered into the benefits of Christ's redemptive work.[ix]

We see, then, that this perspective on adoption has assigned to us both the rights (authority over resources) and responsibilities of an executive in God's family business. As such, God calls us to use our minds in the employment of the resources He has entrusted to us in order to advance His agenda. As emphasized throughout this book, the focal point of that agenda is maximum agape production. Through the Holy Spirit, who dwells within us as a result of the New Covenant, we receive the necessary intellectual guidance to understand and apply Scripture in order to achieve that objective.

The apostle Paul describes the spiritual insight provided by the Holy Spirit in 1 Corinthians 2:12: "Now we have received not the spirit of the world, but the Spirit who is from God, that we might understand the things freely given us by God." Notice what this verse does not say. Paul does not say that we have received the Holy Spirit who will prompt our emotions to guide us. Rather, he indicates that God gives the Holy Spirit "that we might understand."

He concludes this chapter that focuses on the ministry of the Holy Spirit by asserting, "But we have the mind of Christ." The Holy Spirit gives us the capacity to see and evaluate situations as Christ would. This possession of the "mind of Christ," the capacity to understand and apply Scripture, does not refer so much to the ability to identify a given chapter and verse pertaining to a situation, but rather it is describing the

Holy Spirit imparting an integrated working knowledge of the principles of Scripture as a whole that enables us to answer the question, "What would Jesus do?"

I want to again assert that I believe that the Holy Spirit even today at times communicates to people through all of the means described above such as direct communication, signs, and the urging of emotions. We see examples of this type of guidance in Scripture, and I have heard too many godly people recount God's use of each of these means of communication in their own lives and ministries to doubt that the Holy Spirit employs these methods of communication today. My point in this chapter, however, has been that these do not constitute the norm for the Holy Spirit's guidance for the myriad decisions confronting us on a daily basis, but instead He primarily utilizes the mind saturated by the principles of Scripture applied to the situations of life to achieve the objective of maximizing agape output.

When we do sense that God is guiding us through signs or promptings, how do we know if we should follow them? Two good questions to ask are: 1) Are these indicators leading in a direction compatible with Scripture? 2) Do I have unshakable confidence that the Holy Spirit is communicating through them? Affirmative answers to both of these questions place us on solid footing.

Our Responsibilities in Seeking Guidance

As already noted, guidance comes primarily through the application of the *principles* of Scripture to the choices confronting us. Therefore, thorough acquaintance with and skill in the application of biblical principles comprise core factors in this process.

Developing this knowledge and the facility for applying Scripture cannot be achieved merely by reading brief daily devotionals. Though these might be great for an appetizer or dessert, the main course needs to be in-depth Bible study. This requires substantial time. Though Scripture does not identify how much time we should devote to Bible study, and no doubt that differs from person to person, it should be long enough for us to systematically and meaningfully engage with a passage of Scripture. I find that a free Bible study program such as e-sword (www.e-sword.net) or a website such as Bible Hub (www.biblehub.com) provide a wealth of tools that support serious Bible study. I also encourage creating a Word file for every book of the Bible to keep notes on your findings as you study. Doing so allows you to compile information and insights for future access.

Needless to say, new believers cannot achieve this objective overnight, which makes it imperative that they seek input from more experienced believers in making decisions. Likewise, none of us have developed a comprehensive knowledge of Scripture or an infallible capacity to apply it, and therefore in making major decisions we all would be wise to seek counsel from others who possess a solid grasp of Scripture and skill in its application.

In decision-making, we also have a responsibility to investigate thoroughly the options available to us. I have witnessed believers seeking to discover the optimal course of action without doing the necessary research. They spent substantial time in prayer but did not research the available options sufficiently to pray intelligently. Instead, they expected the Holy Spirit to compensate for their lack of diligence, i.e. to guide them without their having done the work of a good CEO. They attempted to delegate up.

In God's design, He has provided us with the capability to discover salient principles of Scripture and also to glean essential facts related to the options available to us. It is only as we meet our responsibility of doing this groundwork that we can expect the Holy Spirit to provide us with optimal guidance. As we do our part, we can be assured that our partner, the Holy Spirit, will do His.

The Holy Spirit's Guidance through Our Minds and Our Role as CEO

The discussion above regarding how the Holy Spirit

provides guidance is crucial to our understanding of our role as CEO. Should the Holy Spirit predominantly provide guidance through direct communication, signs, or emotional promptings, rather than through our minds, our role would be reduced to that of an Old Testament believer or even beneath that. That arrangement would diminish our responsibilities to merely waiting for the direct communication, sign, or prompting, and then enacting it.

Imagine a board of directors telling a new CEO that the company has a chief operating officer, Pete, who is extremely intelligent, knows everything about the business and makes infallible decisions. As a result, the board informs the CEO that he only needs to follow all of Pete's input in order to succeed. The new CEO would then ask, "Why do you need me? Why not just let Pete run your company?" They respond that Pete lacks the outgoing personality to assume that role. Therefore, they need a CEO who will serve as a figurehead to implement Pete's decisions.

This new CEO is CEO in title only. In effect he has no authority or responsibility. He has no opportunity or need to employ his mind and use his skills. At one level, this position would be very comfortable, but it would also be fictitious.

God has created us in His image and called us to function as His stewards, managing the resources of our lives to advance his purposes. He has given us the Holy Spirit to provide guidance through our thought processes. Under the New Covenant, the Holy Spirit does not replace us as CEO of our lives but provides guidance through our thought processes so that we can succeed at that role.

Our Need for Power

We not only need the Holy Spirit to give guidance to our minds in order to function effectively as CEO, but we also need Him to provide strength for our wills in order to implement those decisions. Success as CEO of our lives requires that we access both the guidance and the power of the Holy Spirit. God's means for our tapping into that power is the topic of the next chapter.

Principle #6
Access Power
from the Holy Spirit

Though Joe was a disciplined person, he also realized his human vulnerabilities. After his first month on the job, some character weaknesses began to surface. He realized that if he did not deal with them soon, they would cause serious trouble.

The first one came in the form of a cute, friendly, well-proportioned 28-year-old single girl who worked in the marketing department. As it happened, the path to Joe's office door went right past her desk. Their friendship began merely as natural interaction. Because Katie was outgoing and happy, it was just natural for Joe to stop at her desk each morning and exchange pleasantries. Given how attractive and outgoing she was, Joe was amazed that she was still unattached. Ultimately she told him that she had been in a serious relationship but had broken it off several months earlier. Joe could tell that she enjoyed his attention.

By the third week, Joe realized how much he looked forward to those conversations. It occurred to him that if this relationship continued to develop, he would lose the respect of other employees and could even destroy his marriage. Yet, each morning found him stopping at her desk and the relationship growing.

Another test of his integrity came from the company softball team, which had won the league championship the previous three years. Shortly after Joe took over as CEO, Ralph, the coach, dropped into Joe's office to inform him that it was a company tradition to let the softball team leave work an hour early on Tuesdays and Thursdays to practice for the Friday night game. He made the point that these employees were giving their time to represent the company on Friday nights, and therefore it was only fair to give them a little time off two days a week for practice. Besides, these practice times gave them the edge, allowing them to honor the company with a winning team.

Ralph ramped up his efforts to get Joe's okay by recruiting some of the other workers to lobby for him. Joe sensed a soft coup brewing that had to be addressed, but like most people, he wanted to be liked and hated confrontation. In addition, he especially wanted to avoid conflict this soon into his new position. Yet he knew that dealing with this situation firmly but appropriately would establish his leadership, and failure to do so would merely attract more challenges.

One of Joe's strengths was also his weakness. As CEO he was driven to succeed, but he had assigned such high priority to work that he was failing to meet his responsibilities as a husband and father. His family knew that it was necessary for Joe to invest extra time in order to get a handle on his new job, but now, as he started his second month, the time had come for him to spend more time at home.

Joe knew that he had to look to his partner, the Holy Spirit, to provide the strength necessary to deal with these issues. He was also aware that the process for acquiring that strength required his participation. He was confident that as he did his part, the Holy Spirit would be faithful in doing His, resulting in Joe gaining the strength to deal successfully with these and other situations confronting him.

Power Available

Managing our lives to optimize agape requires the discipline to overcome internal desires and external pressures that pull us in counterproductive directions. We also need the corresponding discipline required to practice productive behaviors. This is especially the case since we are seeking to produce agape and our fallen natures possess a strong inclination toward selfishness. Even as believers we experience powerful proclivities toward selfishness, and consequently displaying agape requires discipline.

Since God is all-powerful, and the Holy Spirit is my business partner, it seems that He could and should supply me with infinite power to deal with the forces seeking to carry me in unloving directions. As a born-again believer, having received a new nature, should not the Holy Spirit have fixed these problems—infused me with sufficient power to overcome them? Shouldn't I be a superhero?

The Need for Power

Even the presence of the Holy Spirit in believers does not make agape production spontaneous. In other words, in many if not most situations, we do not automatically display agape. We find proof of this in our own lives and that of other believers. Though we possess the Holy Spirit, we maintain an inclination to think, speak, and behave selfishly. When someone pushes ahead of us in line at the supermarket, we tend to feel irritated and to think unkind thoughts. Anyone who doubts that believers possess strong selfish inclinations has never attended a church business meeting or done marriage counseling with two Christians.

Overcoming these selfish proclivities found even in believers requires that we actively access the power of the Holy Spirit. In God's design, the Holy Spirit makes power available to us, but, as with guidance, appropriating that power requires that we engage in the process. We can be confident that the Holy Spirit will do his part if we do ours.

Promise of Power

God designed the Christian life to be infused with supernatural power. That power is available to manifest itself in the two forms of agape production described earlier: 1) Being the person God designed us to be: 2) Accomplishing the things God designed us to achieve.

2 Timothy 1:7 assures us of the capacity of the Holy Spirit to transform our personalities: "(F)or God gave us a spirit not of fear but of power and love and self-control." The Holy Spirit empowers us to exercise the self-control required to resist selfish behaviors and maintain an agape-oriented personality. Most if not all of us struggle with self-control in some area of our lives. That weakness differs for each of us, but regardless of what form it takes, if we do not employ the power of the Holy Spirit to control it, it will destroy us.

We all know about David's sin with Bathsheba, but as we read about David's life we realize that this sin was only the culmination of a lifestyle of weakness in David's relationship with women. The law stipulated that kings should not have many wives, but Scripture indicates that in every phase of his life, David kept collecting more of them. Though Scripture does not record that God dealt with David regarding his many marriages, this weakness in his relationships with women ultimately caught up with him in his relationship with Bathsheba, devastating virtually every aspect of his life. The good news for us is that as New Testament believers we enjoy a special provision of power from the Holy Spirit, which, as we appropriate it, will enable us to exercise self-control in every area of our lives.

Acts 1:8 promises power in regard to accomplishing the tasks God designed us to achieve: "But you will receive power when the Holy Spirit has come upon you, and you will be my witnesses in Jerusalem and in all Judea and Samaria, and to the end of the earth." Jesus charged His disciples with the daunting assignment of spreading the gospel in the midst of a nation that recently demanded His crucifixion and throughout a larger secular world that mandated the worship of Caesar. We read in Scripture and history how that fledgling early church, empowered by the Holy Spirit, evangelized that hostile world. The Holy Spirit likewise can empower us in the exercise of our spiritual gifts to achieve His purposes.

The Process for Appropriating Power

This leads us to the question, Exactly what is our part in the process of appropriating the power of the Holy Spirit? We get a clue to the answer by considering the two factors required to gain physical strength: food and exercise.

Food

Appropriating spiritual strength requires spiritual food. Though the Holy Spirit has infinite power, in God's design He unleashes His power in our lives through our ingestion of spiritual food. The food through which the Holy Spirit imparts strength is Scripture. We tend to think of Scripture only as a source of information, i.e. "light." and it certainly is that. However, the Bible also channels "life," spiritual strength, into our lives.

Jesus taught, "It is the Spirit who gives life; the flesh is no help at all. The words that I have spoken to you are spirit and life." (John 6:63) Likewise, we read in Hebrews 4:12, "For the word of God is living and active, sharper than any two-edged sword, piercing to the division of soul and of spirit, of joints and of marrow, and discerning the thoughts and intentions of the heart." The Greek word translated "active" is the source for the English word "energy." Scripture possesses the capacity to provide us with spiritual life and energy.

J.J. Watt, defensive end for the Houston Texans is 6'5" and all muscle. The Texan fans love him. Quarterbacks not so much. One article reported that he consumes a 7000 calorie diet. I am not recommending that. I'm just saying. Imagine, however, that J.J. Watt had reduced his total diet to one Panera Bread scone every meal. It would not take long before he deteriorated into a shell of the man he is now. The fans would no longer cheer for him and quarterbacks would like him a lot more.

Daily scriptural intake of a brief devotional comprises the spiritual equivalent of the scone diet. Scones are good, and it is great to enjoy them on occasion. However, they are not adequate to serve as our primary diet. By way of contrast, taking in 7000 calories of Scripture on a regular basis can transform you into a spiritual J.J. Watt, generating the strength you need to take on the challenges of life.

The approach to Scripture for the purpose of accessing the life, the empowerment of the Holy Spirit, differs somewhat from its study for the purpose of deriving light, i.e. guidance. Ingesting Scripture to derive power requires that we think more in terms of application. It is possible to read Scripture with a focus on gleaning knowledge that overlooks its message related to our lifestyle. Reading for application requires a degree of intentionality. We must look for the implications relative to our values and behaviors and must consciously query ourselves regarding how well we are making the applications.

A nurse observed some doctors, well acquainted with the health hazards resulting from cigarettes, head outside to smoke during their breaks. They displayed a breakdown between knowledge and application. Empowerment by the Holy Spirit through the Word comes as we ask while reading Scripture, "Does my life reflect this truth? If not, when and how am I going to apply it?" The Jewish leaders at the time of Christ displayed this breakdown between knowledge and application.

Meditation comprises an especially potent way to absorb spiritual nutrients from Scripture. As we memorize and reflect on Scripture, it tends to release its power. An especially effective way to achieve this is through meditating on the implications of each word or phrase in a verse.

"(D)o not be anxious about anything, but in everything by prayer and supplication with thanksgiving let your requests be made known to God." (Philippians 4:6)

- "Do not be anxious:" That sounds like a command. Am I obeying it? Am I anxious? Why am I anxious? How should I deal with my anxiety?
- "About anything:" That seems pretty comprehensive. Paul doesn't leave exceptions, no wiggle room.
- "But in everything:" The word "but" seems to indicate that Paul is about to give the cure for anxiety. What is it? Am I taking the cure? Another one of those all-inclusive statements. What is Paul saying that I should do about everything?
- "By prayer and supplication:" Paul seems to be saying that prayer and supplication provide the cure for anxiety. Am I anxious about situations because I am not committing them to the Lord in prayer? What is the difference between prayer and supplication? It sounds like Paul is telling me to pray about everything. How do I do that? Am I doing that?
- "With thanksgiving:" I have a lot to be thankful for. How thankful am I? Do I express my gratitude to the Lord in prayer? If I focused on my blessings in prayer and expressed my gratitude, would that improve my outlook on life—reduce my anxiety and give me more power?
- "Let your requests be made known to God:" That sounds like another imperative. What a great thing that the God of the universe actually commands me to come to Him with my requests. It sounds like asking God for things is not imposing on Him but something He wants me to do.

The few thoughts given for each phrase above represent only the tip of the iceberg. It is possible to meditate on and think through the implications of just one scriptural phrase for a long time, a process that enables us to fully digest its meaning and applications to our lives. Digesting Scripture in this way is very much like chewing our food. Just as we do not swallow our food whole, likewise, this type of meditation enables us to derive the nutrients from a passage.

A good means of developing spiritual muscle is selecting a verse for each day to memorize and meditate on throughout the day. We can ruminate over the verse, one word or phrase at a time, especially during those mental downtimes when work or other activities do not demand the use of our brain, like when we are mowing the lawn, driving, or going to sleep. This is a good practice especially because it is during these mental downtimes that our thoughts tend to be unmanaged and get us into trouble. Instead of those negative outcomes, we can derive spiritual strength through meditation. I am frequently amazed as the Lord reveals some significant spiritual truth as I reflect on a word or phrase that did not seem to have any more to offer. It seems that Scripture always has more to give as we continue to meditate on it.

Exercise

Scripture has a fair amount to say about exercise. In 1 Timothy 4:7 Paul instructs Timothy (and us): "...exercise yourself toward godliness." (NKJV) The Greek word for exercise provides the source for the English word "gymnasium." Paul is challenging us to work out in God's spiritual gymnasium.

Exercising spiritual disciplines in our lifestyle and ministry produces two positive results. The most obvious one is found in the practical output. If I discipline myself to be godly, my family and friends benefit. If I discipline myself in ministry, for example employing the gift of helps, the people I help will benefit.

Not as obvious but nonetheless very important is the second benefit, the development of spiritual muscle. Paul describes that outcome as follows:

> Not only that, but we rejoice in our sufferings, knowing that suffering produces endurance, and endurance produces character, and character produces hope, (Romans 5:3-4)

In essence he is telling us that as we respond biblically to the challenges of life, we become stronger—we develop spiritual muscle. Next time around we will possess the strength to face even greater temptations without giving in—to minister in even more difficult situations and not respond unbiblically or quit.

James conveys a similar message:

> Consider it all joy, my brethren, when you encounter various trials, knowing that the testing of your faith produces endurance. And let endurance have its perfect result, so that you may be perfect and complete, lacking in nothing. (James 1:2-4 NASB)

James assures us that as we exercise ourselves in dealing with the challenges of life biblically through the power of the Holy Spirit we will become "perfect and complete," that is, every muscle group will become developed. Not only will we be able to do spiritual bench presses but also squats and curls. We will even develop the conditioning to be good at cardio.

Earlier in my Christian life when I read this passage my response was "Really? Count it all joy when I find myself confronted with hard times?" But one day while I was at the gym the message finally sank in. We pay to belong to a gym in order to develop physical strength. An effective workout is strenuous and even painful. No pain, no gain. Or as my nephew likes to say regarding the discomfort produced by working out, "Pain is just weakness leaving the body." When we encounter trials, God is providing a spiritual gym for us free of charge! We can sit on the spiritual weight bench, look at the free weights, think about how bad lifting them will make us feel, and pity ourselves, or we can do our maximum number of bench presses ever, and then do one more.

The Holy Spirit uses this kind of spiritual exercise to enable us to develop spiritual muscle. Yes, He has infinite power, but God has chosen this method for transmitting that strength to us. So the next time someone cuts you off in traffic, or your printer runs out of ink when you are hurrying to get out a report, or the dog actually does eat your homework, just realize that the Holy Spirit, your partner—and trainer, wants you to do a few bench presses so you can build up a little more spiritual muscle.

Viewing life from that perspective can be challenging. It requires thinking about life through the lens of faith rather than through the glasses of sight.

When I get stuck in a traffic jam, as I feel frustration building, I find myself having this conversation with myself: "Okay Paul, right now you are at a dead standstill and have been for the past five minutes with no prospect of anything changing. This apparently is God's plan for you right now. Do you have a better plan? Are you smarter than He is? Are you going to advise Him on the deficiencies of His plan and how yours is superior?" By the time I finish that conversation I usually have a better perspective on the traffic jam. I even find myself able to rejoice in the reality that this situation is God's very best for me, a means of helping me develop spiritual strength. I take a deep breath, begin to experience His peace, and pursue productive ways to use that time such as praying, singing a song of praise (with the windows closed), meditating on a Bible verse, or thinking through the best way to produce agape in the situation waiting at my destination.

I would like to report that in all the challenges of life I exhibit that faith response, but I am not there yet. I am still not a spiritual J.J Watt. But I am working on the 7000 calorie spiritual diet and trying to do some good work in God's gym. Though I have a long way to go, thanks to my trainer, the Holy Spirit, I am seeing some progress.

Dale Davis, in his excellent daily devotional book, *Draw Me Nearer*, which I would encourage you to get, recounts the visit of a bodybuilder to an African tribe. The chief, impressed with his physique asked what he did with those muscles. He demonstrated to the chief by striking a few poses. The chief responded by asking, "What else do you do with those muscles." The bodybuilder responded, "Well, that's pretty much it," to which the chief responded, "What a waste. What a waste."[x] What does God want us to do with the spiritual muscles we develop through digesting the Word and spiritual exercise? Previous chapters have accentuated that the answer is to produce agape. But how do we maximize agape output? The chapters ahead provide the answer.

Principle #7
Inventory Your Resource Package

As Joe began his second month as CEO of ABC Widget Company, he opened a file that he had been compiling across the past 30 days. Though he knew that the company was in financial trouble, he decided at the outset not to make any impulsive moves but instead to spend the first month carefully assessing the company and its current operation. He had explained this plan to the board, and they had signed off on it.

A major piece of that assessment consisted of inventorying the resources available to him. On the morning of his third day at the company, Joe created a Word file that he simply named "Resources." During the four weeks that followed, he had developed a comprehensive list of the resources available to him for making a profit. He included and described in detail obvious items such as the building and equipment, money in the bank and other financial resources, current supply and product inventories, customer accounts, and the team of skilled employees working in every aspect of the operation from designing widgets to selling them.

Joe spent considerable time looking at financial statements and bank statements, walking the premises, and talking with employees about the equipment. He queried the head of sales about the customer list. By the end of that first month, the "Resources" file provided Joe with the information necessary to begin making management decisions.

Assessing Our Resources

Successfully functioning as CEO of our lives requires that we assess our resources. If you have never systematically appraised the package of resources God has assigned to you, it is probably far more extensive than you realize, which means that your potential for producing agape is far greater than you might have imagined.

Assessment, especially of our capabilities, is more challenging than it might first appear because of their complexities. As we learn more about the intricacies of the DNA molecule, we are beginning to realize how unique and complex we are as human beings. In this chapter we will discover that our package of resources is also highly complex and individualistic. Consequently, seeking to describe it is more of an art than a science, and determining its most profitable employment is vastly more complicated than seeking a square hole in which to fit a square peg. Complex though it may be, maximum profitability requires an accurate assessment of this package of gifts.

This chapter guides us through that assessment. As we consider the various categories of resources we possess that enable us to produce agape, I would encourage you to use the form at Appendix B, or, like Joe, open a Word file, or get out a pad of paper to begin to catalog the resources that you possess. Because of the complexities just mentioned, it will soon become apparent that you cannot create a comprehensive list. However, sketching in major pieces will provide the foundation for managing those resources. Married couples will benefit by working together on this project, since managing and employing your resources necessarily entails a joint effort.

They All Belong to God

The foundational principle underlying the analysis of our package of resources resides in the realization that all we possess belongs to God and is on loan to us for the purpose of producing agape. Our very life is a gift from God. Psalm 100:3 reminds us, "Know that the LORD Himself is God; It is He who has made us, and not we ourselves." In 1 Corinthians 4:7, Paul asked rhetorically, "What do you have that you did not receive?" The obvious answer is nothing. Job recognized that he arrived in this world wearing only his birthday suit (Job 1:21) and therefore in addition to life itself, everything else that he possessed came from the hand of God. The air we breathe, the ground we stand on, and the food we eat all come from and therefore belong to God. As the CEO of a company, we begin with the reality that we manage resources that we do not own.

If a CEO began to view and treat aspects of company resources as belonging to him, this could result in embezzlement and jail time. Though God does not incarcerate us for embezzling His resources, doing so does not turn out well. Functioning as CEO begins with acknowledging that all of our assets belongs to God, and therefore we have a responsibility to catalog them and strategize how we can best use them to produce optimal agape for Him.

Types of Resources

We might place our resources into two categories: our capabilities, i.e. our talents that enable us to produce agape; and other resources such as material possessions and our network of relationships that can be used to benefit others.

Capabilities

Our capabilities include natural and spiritual gifts, natural gifts consisting of those capabilities embedded in our physical makeup at our physical birth while spiritual gifts encompass those bestowed on us by the Holy Spirit at our spiritual birth. In both of these areas, we are distinctly unique as individuals.

While our vastly intricate genetic code reveals the complexity of our physical capabilities, we tend to think of spiritual gifts as simple, generic commodities. We view a person as either having or not having the gift of evangelism or teaching or administration as if the Holy Spirit makes these gifts with a cookie-cutter and dispenses them. She has the gift of teaching and he has the gift of evangelism.

I sense spiritual gifts possess far more detail and variety. Two people may own cars, but one may have a Honda van while the other owns a Mustang convertible. Likewise, two people may possess the gift of evangelism but in all likelihood it will take a distinctly different form for each.

To begin with, as with our natural gifts, the Holy Spirit seems to give spiritual gifts in differing degrees or quantities. The Holy Spirit might bless one believer with a large portion of the gift of evangelism and another with a smaller serving. Virtually all of us can do math to some degree, with most of us having an average capacity that enables us to balance our checkbooks. Others who are especially gifted in math can do differential equations while those at the low end of the spectrum struggle to balance their checkbooks but nonetheless possess enough math skill to get along in life. Likewise, most if not all Christians seem to have the gift of helps, with all of us possessing a different level of gifting in this area. If the pastor asks us to help set up chairs, we probably will not say, "Sorry, I don't have the gift of helps, but Josh does. Ask him." We all can administer or evangelize or teach to some degree, but one person is more gifted in these areas than another. It seems that as with natural gifts, the Holy Spirit distributes the size of the various spiritual gifts He assigns to individuals along a bell curve.

The fact that we have different degrees of gifting adds complexity to our assessment, requiring us to include the "how much" question. The issue is not whether we have the gift of teaching but the size of our teaching gift.

That complexity is further increased by the fact that spiritual gifts not only come in differing quantities but in a wide variety of styles. Two people might both have a substantial quantity of the gift of teaching, with one possessing great skill at teaching kindergarten children while another is gifted at teaching on a graduate level. The kindergarten teacher would probably not be acquainted with the material covered at a graduate level, while the graduate prof's worst nightmare would probably be teaching a group of kindergartners. Both have the same level of gifting but different styles. Consequently, in analyzing our spiritual gifts we not only need to ask "how much" of a certain gift we possess but "what style."

The complexities increase as we seek to untangle natural and spiritual gifts. Is the administrator of a Christian school employing the natural or spiritual gift of administration or both? The same might be asked regarding a Christian doing administration in a public school. It seems that our natural and spiritual gifts blend together to form a combined capability

This combined package of our natural and spiritual gifts constitutes something akin to a capabilities DNA. Just as our physical DNA is highly complex and unique, the same is true of our DNA related to natural and spiritual gifts.

The differing components of this integrated package of competencies enhance one another, thus making the whole greater than the sum of the parts. For example, a person with technical skills plus administrative capabilities may qualify as an executive in a computer or engineering firm.

Our pursuit of the most effective use of this complex, integrated package leads us to ask questions such as what courses did I enjoy most and came easiest for me? At what types of tasks am I most successful doing? What hasn't gone so well? What activities elicit a positive response from people? Which prompt a negative response? What seems natural and what seems forced? Which are fun and which are labored? What ages seem responsive? One on one or groups? Large or small groups? Working by myself or with others? Leading or working as part of a team?

This exploration of our capabilities DNA helps us to discover the types of tasks that achieve maximum agape output for us. The chapter ahead will give this topic further consideration.

Other Resources

In addition to our natural and spiritual capabilities, our resource package also includes a significant list of other assets such as money, possessions such as homes and cars, degrees and certifications, work experience, and our network of relationships. We can employ each of these to produce agape in a variety of ways. For example, we can use our home to care for our family, show hospitality, or serve as a venue for conducting Bible studies.

Though we tend not to think of our family as an agape producing asset, it is to a very significant extent. My wife and I working as a team have produced far more agape than I could have done on my own. My children, now grown, are producing substantial amounts of agape. Therefore, our investment in them turned out to be a major means of agape production. Their children possess the potential of multiplying that investment.

Prayer constitutes a huge resource that we tend to overlook. Prayer does change things, and access to God who wields total control over the universe represents a major means of producing agape. Perhaps the most loving thing we can do for any person is to pray for them.

We can add many other agape producing resources to this list. A working knowledge of this integrated package of resources prepares us to develop a strategy for the optimal employment of our lives, which is the topic of the chapter ahead.

Principle #8
Think Strategically

Joe poured a cup of coffee for himself, walked into his office, shut the door behind him, and took a seat on the couch at the far end of the room where he could begin to collect his thoughts. This was the day that Joe had patiently anticipated for a month. Today he would begin developing a strategic plan for the future of ABC Widget Company.

Joe possessed that great balance between caution and initiative. He had displayed caution in investing a month in fully analyzing the operation of ABC Widget Company, including the development of a comprehensive list of the resources available to him. He resisted the temptation to make impulsive decisions. Now the time had come for him to display initiative.

He realized that he could take a comfortable approach to managing this company by merely fine-tuning the operation in an attempt to make it more profitable. Doing so would require little risk and may even enable him to start turning a profit. But he knew that this safe approach would probably not produce *maximum* profit. Achieving maximum profitability would require that he reassess the entire operation in order to develop an optimal strategy. He would include in that analysis all the options available to him.

This radical reassessment would encompass such considerations as moving the company to another state that had lower taxes, fewer regulations, and lower labor costs. He would consider the production of a wide variety of widgets, calculate the cost of outsourcing various aspects of the operation, think through the advantages of personnel changes, explore the availability of better accounting software, look into the benefits of online sales, and assess the advantages of a wide variety of other possibilities. Of course, he would have to sell his optimal plan to the board, and with their approval implement it with utmost wisdom, caution, and sensitivity toward company personnel.

Joe wanted the assurance that with the resources available to him, the strategy he developed would produce optimal profit. He did not want to look back 10 years from now and reflect, "I sure wish we would have made this or that change a decade ago. In the long run, it would have been a lot more profitable."

As Joe contemplated the number of variables involved in such a plan, he realized that the number of possible configurations for a potential strategy could number in the thousands, if not millions. He could hire personnel, eliminate positions in any or all departments, or transfer individuals from one department to another. He could take money from the budget of one department and give it to another one. He could get rid of equipment, fix it, or buy new models. Many other possibilities came to mind.

The resulting strategy would entail a complex network of decisions, each one influencing the other, with the composite plan having the potential of making or losing money. Armed with these thoughts, Joe was ready to pursue the best possible strategy for ABC Widget Company.

Thinking Strategically

Strategy, initially a military term, is now also employed in the realm of business, which is our application here. At root, strategy refers to the development of a comprehensive plan for the most effective employment of resources in order to achieve an objective. For our discussion, this entails matching our package of resources with the opportunity that will produce maximum agape.

Principle #1, Manage Proactively, stressed the necessity of aggressively managing every area of our lives because chaos is waiting to erode anything not proactively organized. This chapter focuses on management of the bigger picture, developing a comprehensive plan for the totality of our life. While we must engage in the ongoing task of managing the component parts of our existence, it is essential that we set aside time to make a comprehensive survey of the overall direction our life is taking to determine whether we are using it optimally, and if not, to devise a plan that will. Though the various pieces of our life might all be working well, we still might not be producing maximum agape.

Ben and Alyssa

Ben, age 36, has a good IT job with Google. His annual reviews the past four years since he was hired have all been excellent. His wife, Alyssa, age 35, who teaches at Stevens Creek Elementary School in Cupertino, enjoys her job. It is advantageous in many ways that their two children, ages five and seven, attend the same school where she teaches. Ben has developed a budget, and they are living within it and even putting a little aside for the kids' college. They like their church, and life otherwise seems to be going smoothly. They are both proactively managing their resources and making optimal use of them in their present situation.

One evening, however, while out on a date night at Outback Steakhouse, Ben and Alyssa found themselves in one of those big-picture conversations about where they see their lives going. They were both surprised as they came to the realization that maybe their present situation, which seemed to be working well for them, might not be taking them in the optimal direction. Though their combined salaries were substantial, the cost of living in Silicon Valley consumed most of their income. They realized that they could make a lot less living elsewhere and actually enhance their bottom line. Even more important, they wondered whether the Silicon Valley culture provided the best environment to raise their children. Both Ben and Alyssa, grew up in Newton, Kansas, and therefore were sensitized to the difference in values.

This discussion uncovered several factors that prompted them to dream together about the prospects of a better plan. As they began to brainstorm, they realized the wisdom of getting away for a weekend to explore the possibilities. Three weeks later found them about 100 miles north in a nice hotel overlooking the Pacific where they devoted the weekend to sorting through their goals, values, priorities, and potential opportunities for best achieving their objectives. They spent time in prayer, seeking the Lord's guidance regarding the best path for their future. That weekend turned out to be a life-transforming experience for them.

During this discussion, Ben and Alyssa put everything on the table. Though in the long run they may not want to make changes in some of these areas, they were at least willing to consider all the options. Ben toyed with the prospect of going back to school for an MBA while Alyssa wondered about homeschooling the children. They considered moving to areas where IT jobs might be plentiful such as Boston or Austin, Texas. That weekend they concluded that they needed to make a significant change. Ben contacted a headhunter to explore employment prospects.

Three months later the moving van backed up to their house to haul off all of their earthly possessions to Newton, Kansas. Ben had decided against the MBA, but with Google on his resume a fast-growing IT company in Wichita offered him a well-paying job that would cover all their bills, allowing Alyssa to homeschool their children. Parents on both sides of the family were delighted to have their grandchildren nearby. Having Ben and Alyssa there was okay, too. Ben and Alyssa welcomed the free childcare.

An added advantage of this move had to do with an idea Ben had been developing on his own time related to technology for live streaming television programs. He realized that live streaming comprised the cutting edge of the television industry. The concept he was developing would improve and simplify the approach currently used by the major companies in that business. The time he was saving with his new 20-minute commute to Wichita enabled him to focus more on the development of this program.

A year later he completed the live streaming technology, which he was able to sell to Hulu for $5 million. That money changed Ben and Alyssa's lifestyles very little, but instead they invested it, using the interest to support a ministry in Uganda, which had been one of their major goals. This substantial support enabled that ministry to start a Christian school that was educating and discipling many children from impoverished Christian families.

Though their previous lifestyle was working, this new strategy was producing substantially more agape. In addition to supporting the school in Uganda, it put their children in a better environment, it blessed both grandparents and grandchildren, and it gave Alyssa more exposure to and influence with their children. The more relaxed pace lent itself to a more wholesome lifestyle.

Rethinking Everything

In developing a strategy, it is a good idea to put everything on the table in your search for the ultimate configuration for your life, allowing the creative juices to flow freely. What about a different career? Another location, even another country? Another degree in a new field? Working from home? Sending the kids to a different school? Homeschooling? Scaling down and living on less? Starting your own business?

Though it is good to be open to all prospects, staying put also offers significant advantages. The cost of moving is substantial, changing careers often means starting at the bottom. In your current job you know where the landmines are located, while a new job may hold surprises, most of which may not be good. Therefore, any change should offer sufficient benefits to offset the liabilities inherent in change.

Therefore, it is essential that we make all changes thoughtfully and not impulsively, and yet it is also important not to allow fear to paralyze us or an overly-conventional mindset to stifle our creativity. "But none of our family has ever lived more than 25 miles from Lancaster, Pennsylvania." Staying within such artificial boundaries provides a high degree of comfort but prevents us from considering what might be the most profitable option. Imagine looking back and reflecting on missed opportunities resulting solely from failure to consider all the options.

The goal in rethinking everything is maximum agape production. I have observed that the minds of many evangelicals when contemplating that objective begin to think in terms of the pastorate, going to the mission field, or teaching in a Christian school. They sense that these pursuits maximize agape production.

Since this exercise requires imagination, imagine if you engaged in an occupation that earned $200,000 each year (probably not a pastorate), and then through effective management of those resources you were able to contribute 25% of those earnings, or $50,000 annually, to produce agape. In some places in the world, such as India, a native evangelist, who speaks the language and is at home in the culture, can be supported for $1000 per year. That means that $50,000 could support 50 of them.

Or those funds could be invested with an organization such as FARMS International where a grant of about $500 can help a Third World evangelical family begin a business that will lift them out of poverty and help support their local church. That

$50,000 could lift 100 families out of poverty each year. Since 90% of those receiving such grants pay them back, the number of those benefitting from your initial investment would keep multiplying.

Therefore, in pondering ways in which a person can produce maximum agape, earning a substantial salary and managing those funds effectively provides a powerful option. If one becomes a pastor, he can minister to a church, but if instead he enters an occupation that enables him to earn $200,000 per year, he can support 50 pastors in areas of the world where the gospel is largely inaccessible. Or he can lift countless Third World evangelicals out of poverty, enabling them to support their churches and influence their communities. My purpose here is not to minimize the value of pastors but only to make the point that other occupations also possess potential for producing high levels of agape.

While we are imagining, think about the fact that none of the major technological powers in America are headed by evangelicals. Microsoft, Apple, Google, and others all display strong liberal, if not anti-evangelical leanings. The same is true of all of the major social media outlets. Imagine if you could become a force for righteousness in one of these areas. Or what if you got into medical research and the Lord used you to discover a cure for a disease. Just yesterday I talked with a young man who is engaged in cutting-edge medical research dealing with potential cures so fantastic that they boggle the mind. What phenomenal means for producing agape! And those ideas just represent the tip of the iceberg.

Previously I have made the point that virtually every occupation provides the potential for producing abundant agape—being a really good electrician, mom, accountant, Congressman, hospice nurse, or first responder can produce large quantities of agape. Consequently, in pursuing the strategy that will produce maximum agape, many career options with significant agape-producing potential present themselves to us, and other opportunities not included in our careers add to that potential.

Paul Johnson, in his *A History of the American People,* [xi] makes the point that in the developmental years of our nation people immigrating to America enjoyed many career opportunities not available to them in the Old Country. On that count, America has not changed, except for the better. I recall Dinesh D'Souza saying that he loved America because it opened up opportunities for him that were inaccessible to him in India. Managing our lives for optimal profit calls us to take advantage of this opportunity for vocational mobility.

The same holds true for the variety of educational options accessible in our society. Also advantageous is the latitude for making career changes at almost any point in life. People frequently switch career objectives in college, in graduate school, early in their careers, at midpoint, and even when they retire. In all these ways and more, we actually do live in the "land of the free," and often this freedom opens the door for greater agape production.

In pursuing the optimal opportunity, a major factor in decision-making is found in our material and other resources discussed in the previous chapter. For example, financial assets may make possible the option of starting a business. The directions we consider should reflect the totality of our collage of capabilities and also our financial and other material resources.

A major tragedy I have observed resides in an unwillingness of some people to consider any option outside the path, perhaps the rut, in which they currently find themselves. This inclination is especially tragic when their current situation is not strongly supported by their set of gifts and is not proving to be especially fruitful. They trudge on, nonetheless, believing that known drudgery and minimal success is better than uncharted waters. Or some are stuck in their current situation merely because they never take the initiative to consider alternatives.

I would challenge you to set aside a couple of hours, start with a clean slate, and see if you can begin to develop a strategy more productive than your current one. If you discover that you are already in the ultimate situation, the exercise gives you the confidence of knowing that. However, such an exercise could transform your life.

The Process for Producing a Strategy

The process of developing a strategy simply consists of looking for the unique niche God has designed for us among the many opportunities available to us. Ephesians 2:10 indicates that God has designed us for specific tasks and those tasks for us. "For we are his workmanship, created in Christ Jesus for good works, which God prepared beforehand, that we should walk in them." Consequently, when we land in that spot, we can be assured of a good fit. And that good fit will produce both external fruitfulness and internal fulfillment. It is a great feeling to be in the place God designed for us.

Though this description of the essence of strategy development makes it seem simple, applying this formula can be highly challenging because of the complexity of our package of resources and the variety of opportunities for employing them.

We are not like a can opener. If yours breaks, you go out and buy a new one, a job a wife might even trust her husband to achieve. We are more like dining room chandeliers. Your kids are playing ball inside and break yours. You might be upset except you never liked it and were looking for an excuse to get a new one. Unlike buying a can opener, thousands of different styles of dining room chandeliers are available, and it seems that only one perfectly matches your tastes, décor, lighting needs, and budget. Not a job to be delegated to a husband. You spend hours in stores and online until you discover the one that uniquely fits your situation. Likewise, our package of resources uniquely equips us for a distinctive agape-producing situation.

The church needs a teacher for a class. You are a teacher. Therefore, they assume you fit that slot. That reflects a can opener mentality.

Instead, determining whether this need for a teacher is a good fit for you parallels selecting a dining room chandelier, prompting many questions. What age group? What class size? What is the topic? When and where does it meet? What is the objective of the class? What is the profile of the anticipated attendee? Does the topic require a specific educational background or type of experience, e.g. does it deal with people struggling financially or divorce care? These and many other factors suggest a chandelier approach to matching your resources with this opportunity. If this level of complexity exists in deciding on a teaching opportunity at the church, how many more variables exist in considering the direction for our whole life?

Recently I heard about Jim, who owns a company that does residential and commercial electrical work. He hires young men who are in the early stages of recovery from drug addiction and helps them get stabilized. He has Bible studies with them first thing in the morning, and throughout the day he works alongside ones needing additional mentoring, discipling them while they install breaker boxes together. This arrangement provides a stable job for these men as they go through the recovery process, gives them a spiritual foundation that empowers them to succeed, and teaches them a trade that will provide a future career. Jim's unique strategy for agape production holds the prospect of maximum output. In addition to his agape production at work, he also bears fruit as a husband, father, neighbor, and church member. In addition, he produces agape through giving financially.

Jim's strategy provides a challenge to us all because it is so creative. Of course, the standard-type opportunities might provide us with the optimal strategy for our lives, but if we think outside of the box, as Jim did, we might discover a unique opportunity that will fit our package of gifts even better.

This special ministry appears to be Jim's niche. He possesses the package of unique gifting required for this unusual approach to agape production. It necessitates skill at business and electrical work, an understanding of Scripture and the ability to communicate it, the personality to supervise a challenging population, the capacity to mentor them, administrative skills to keep the plan running, some startup capital, a significant amount of practical wisdom and patience, a supportive family, and numerous other resources. Consequently, Jim's capabilities and other resources uniquely qualify him for this means of agape production.

Some Bible scholars reject the view that God has a perfect spot for the investment of our package of gifts. Instead, they believe that it could be used equally as effectively in many places, and we might choose any of them. However, in light of the fact that the Lord has the hairs of our head numbered, which for some of us requires constant recalculation, that He is working all things together for our good, and that we consistently encounter divine appointments, we can have a high degree of confidence that God has created a specific situation for the optimal utilization of our unique package of gifts. In addition, Ephesians 2:10, the verse quoted earlier, suggests that God has designed us to achieve specific tasks, and He has designed those tasks for us.

Wintley Phipps tells the story that early in his career as a gospel singer, while on a flight he noticed that the flight attendant seemed to be having a difficult day. In an attempt to cheer her up, he gave her one of his recordings. Three weeks later, that attendant recognized Cliff Barrows as he boarded her flight. She greeted him and then asked if he had ever heard of a singer named Wintley Phipps. When he indicated that he had not, she gave him the recording. Three weeks after that, Wintley Phipps received a call from Cliff Barrows inviting him to be a soloist for the Billy Graham Crusades. Wintley Phipps refers to this sort of connection as a "hookup from heaven."[xii] Our search for the ultimate strategy for our lives occurs in the context of a supernatural environment. God has a plan for us, and the Holy Spirit is engaged in guiding our minds to lead us to that strategy. As CEO of our lives, we have a responsibility to do our part in this process.

Sorting through Options

Earlier I made a case from Scripture that the Holy Spirit

predominantly guides us through our thought processes as we prayerfully seek to apply the principles of Scripture to the opportunities available to us. A great challenge related to the development of a strategy resides in the fact that Scripture does not provide specific guidance for many issues related to our strategy development. The job in Dallas and the one in Tulsa are very similar in many respects. How does having the mind of Christ lead us to the optimal choice in that situation?

Earlier I stressed the necessity of doing research into the full range of opportunities accessible to us. As we apply the principles of Scripture in evaluating the most promising options, we usually discover that given our skill set and other resources only a few options represent prime candidates for optimal agape production.

I find that prayer virtually always enables me to grasp the "mind of Christ" in choosing from among these options. It is essential to be in prayer throughout the strategy development process. However, our prayers become more focused as we approach a final selection. As I talk through the various elements related to a decision with the Lord, I find that He directs my mind toward salient issues that confirm the superiority of a given option and eliminate others.

Note my mention of *talking through* the decision with the Lord. Some people fail to receive answers through prayer because they confine their prayer effort merely to asking God to show them the best option. I do not believe that this approach is especially fruitful. Rather, we need to *converse* with the Lord in detail about the options confronting us.

We might feel that since the Lord knows everything about everything anyway, we do not need to discuss the details with Him. But despite the fact that He does know everything, He calls us to talk over our challenges with Him. Prayers in Scripture often include information that God already knows but which the one praying rehearses with Him anyway.

A good way of developing a discussion approach to prayer entails imagining you are explaining to a friend the decision confronting you. In doing so, you would describe the prime options on your list, the pros and cons of each, and your reasons for the direction you are currently leaning. I find that as I engage in this type of discussion with the Lord, the Holy Spirit draws my attention to compelling issues that become deciding factors. For example, the Holy Spirit might direct my thoughts to the realization that the job in St. Louis requires more sales ability than I possess.

Notice that this process does not entail gaining a subjective feeling toward one option or the other, but rather its goal is to glean insights from the Lord that direct our minds toward the optimal alternative. Almost always as I discuss options with the Lord, I come away confident regarding the best choice and the reasons why it is superior.

Strategizing As a Way of Life

In business personnel move, the market changes, the government introduces new regulations, and the economy goes through cycles. We experience the same changing scenery in our own lives. We change, our resources change, situations change, and also we are constantly learning. Therefore, our strategy needs to be a work in progress throughout life.

Across the years, this process has enabled me to develop a more refined perspective on the types of activities I can and cannot do effectively. This knowledge has helped me hone my strategy by eliminating initiatives in less productive areas and pursuing ones that promise greater profit.

The demand for continuously updating our comprehensive strategy and subsidiary strategies results in strategy development and application becoming a way of life. We need to be thinking strategically about virtually every aspect of our life on an ongoing basis.

A potential pitfall of a strategic focus resides in the danger of living in the future instead of the present. An effective strategic approach to life requires that we plan for the future while living in the present. Since we can only implement our strategy in the present, living strategically requires that we make the most of today.

Succeeding as CEO requires that we effectively implement

our strategy. The chapter ahead considers some of the most critical issues in applying our strategy to real life.

Principle #9
Optimize Resource
Distribution

After Joe developed and implemented his new strategy, all went
well for a while. Soon, however, various challenges confronting
the company required that Joe reallocate money and other
resources in order to achieve optimal performance.

Doing so was difficult since all of the needy areas he
identified had valid claims on available resources. Research and
development wanted to start working on a new type of widget,
which they believed would keep the company ahead of the
competition but would also require significant capital to
develop. Equipment needed updating and the shop foreman
noted that an extra person in production could boost output

substantially. The sales department made the case that their limited travel budget prevented them from covering potentially profitable territories.

Meeting these needs would require no management skill whatever if the company had sufficient resources to cover them all. However, despite the recent boost in sales resulting from Joe's new strategy, it would require a year or so before the company built up substantial working capital.

In addition, Joe realized that management would require a lot less expertise if he could focus just on one area and let the others ride. He knew, though, that if one area of the operation failed, the whole company would go down. If production thrived but sales tanked, the company would be spending money without making money. If research and development did not keep up with the market, the competition would cut into their market share. Failure to do accurate accounting would lead to bad decisions and potential bankruptcy. Consequently, he had to distribute the resources available to him in a way that would keep every aspect of the company functioning most effectively.

Distributing Resources

Earning maximum profit requires the most effective distribution of our resources. As Joe concluded, if we had at our disposal unlimited resources, management would be easy. However, none of us do, thus requiring that we distribute those that we have most effectively.

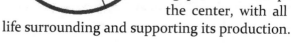

This distribution challenge might best be portrayed by this diagram, which depicts some areas demanding resources. Real life includes many additional areas not listed in this diagram. Since God calls us to manage our lives to maximize agape, the chart positions agape at the center, with all other aspects of life surrounding and supporting its production.

As with Joe, we soon realize that all of these aspects of life must be kept afloat. If our health declines, all other aspects of agape production will slow down or come to a halt. The fracturing of our family would not only hinder the flow of agape to family members but would also drain our finances, emotions, time, and other resources, eroding all aspects of agape production. If we fail to give adequate attention to our job, we could find ourselves unemployed, which would negatively influence agape production in every area. Letting our spiritual life deteriorate would not only diminish our capacity to produce agape but also our desire to do so.

Some distributions of our resources are more profitable than others. If a man was devoting an hour to relaxation beyond that which he needed, and at the same time his son could use some help with a school project, transferring that hour from relaxation to spending time helping his son would no doubt produce more agape. Optimal productivity requires our ongoing tweaking of resource distribution for maximum productivity. If we are tight on time but have a little excess in our finances, we might pay someone to mow the grass or clean the house. (This option exchanges money for time. When necessary, we can also exchange time for money through various means.) If things are going well at work but challenges are developing at home, we might transfer some time in that direction. Likewise, if we feel ourselves getting a little wobbly spiritually, added time for Bible study and prayer might be advised. More than normal stress or a feeling of futility about life might call for investing time and money in an extended vacation.

The believer enjoys the special blessing of knowing that God provides us with all of the resources required for every situation, and therefore we will always be able to meet our essential needs with the resources available to us. If it seems that our resources are insufficient to cover everything, the situation may call us to proactive management that raises questions such as: Are all the demands on our resources actual needs? Should I pursue increasing resources—selling assets, a second job, etc.? Does my comprehensive strategy need tweaking?

Distributing resources represents one of the most challenging aspects of being a CEO. This is one reason companies hire managers and not robots. This challenge, however, also comprises an enjoyable element of managing our lives. It is fun to figure out how we can distribute the resources available to us to meet demands and optimize output. Doing so is especially enjoyable knowing that the Lord has provided us with all of the resources needed to achieve His purposes. We just need to figure out how to use them most effectively.

Though no pat formula exists for distributing resources, the principles that follow can be helpful.

Find the Sweet Spot in Dealing with Conflicting Objectives

An analysis of virtually every aspect of life reveals that for every objective a legitimate opposing objective exists. I want to be kind and generous with my children but I do not want to pamper them. I want our home to be organized, but I also want the freedom to live in it, which will result in some things getting out of place. I want to maintain a healthy diet, but I do not want my diet to consume my life, examining every label for nefarious ingredients. I want to be friendly with employees, but I still want them to be responsive to my authority.

Some have expressed this truth with the cliché, "The devil is in the ditches." He wants to draw us into imbibing in too much of a good thing, which will make it a bad thing. Moving too far in either direction creates problems. In fact, it creates a double problem because I will have an unhealthy fixation toward one extreme while failing to derive the benefits from the opposite objective. Being overly generous with my children can incline them toward materialism and at the same time deprive them of learning self-denial and deferred gratification.

A major management challenge in distributing our resources most effectively entails guarding against moving toward one extreme to the exclusion of the opposing objective. We avoid this by identifying conflicting objectives and finding the sweet spot, the optimal agape-producing midpoint that most effectively integrates the two.

Often some breakdown in our strategy signals that we have strayed from the sweet spot and have moved too far toward one extreme. If we are having health issues, perhaps we have moved too far toward succeeding at work and need to give more attention to diet and exercise. Finding the sweet spot in dealing with conflicting objectives promotes optimal agape production.

I have discovered that most of life's issues have a natural optimal sweet spot. There seems to be a natural, healthy weight for my body. Being careless about diet and exercise results in my weight going above it. However, to go below it requires excessive work and attention. As much as I'd like to have six-pack abs, in seeking to maximize agape I cannot justify the cost in time and effort. But neither do I want to settle for a keg! For me, seven hours of sleep is optimal. Getting fewer erodes health and optimal functioning. Getting more unnecessarily consumes time and leaves me feeling sluggish.

We were able to purchase an optimal home. A larger one would have resulted in our paying for space that we do not need, but a smaller one would have left us cramped. We have enough yard for attractive landscaping but not so much that its upkeep makes unnecessary demands on our time or funds. Managing our lives for optimal agape output requires identifying and occupying the sweet spot in every area of life.

Care for the Goose That Lays the Golden Eggs

You may not prefer to think of yourself as a goose, but in this case the analogy fits. Since your capabilities represent the prime mechanism for producing profit, it is essential that your resource distribution includes caring for personal needs. Though it is legitimate to neglect some personal needs temporarily to deal with emergencies or meet special challenges such as crashing for finals or a sickness in the family, any plan that does not care for our long-term personal physical, emotional, and spiritual well-being will not produce maximum agape, because it will kill the goose laying the agape, or at least make him or her sick and ineffective. Getting optimal sleep, necessary exercise and recreation, and essential time for reading Scripture, prayer, and church attendance must be components of any good strategy.

It is essential for each of us to determine the optimal time and other resources required for meeting personal needs since they are different for all of us. When I was in college, I read that Hudson Taylor got up at 4 AM for prayer time. For an alarm clock, the Chinese would light a piece of punk and place it between their toes. When it burned down to their toes, it would wake them up. That was Hudson Taylor's means of getting awake for this devotional time. Wanting to develop the spiritual qualities Hudson Taylor exhibited, I decided to adopt his practice for gleaning spiritual input. I didn't do the punk thing but instead set my alarm for 4 AM. After about two days, I had to push myself through every activity and was failing to get required tasks done. It soon became apparent that Hudson Taylor's physical makeup and mine were not the same. I had to find an approach to my spiritual development that corresponded to my DNA.

Not so negotiable is a day of rest each week. Some point out that the New Testament does not include a commandment to keep the Sabbath. However, others have observed that God has designed us to need one day of rest each week, and failure to take it will reduce our productivity.

At one point in my life, an older man, apparently observing that I was failing at this discipline, took me aside and told me his own story. He was working at retail sales seven days per week. A Christian co-worker told him that if he took a day off, his weekly sales would actually increase. He initiated that practice and his sales did increase. I got the message.

One of the many bad ideas coming out of the French Revolution resided in their creation of a calendar that provided for a day of rest every ten days. This calendar only survived for a little over 12 years.

It is interesting that God required the Israelites to take time off to gather at Jerusalem three times each year: a week in the spring, a day in the summer, and about three weeks in the fall (if they stayed in Jerusalem for all of the fall holy days).

Of special interest is the requirement to use one of their tithes as sort of a vacation fund, to buy whatever would bring joy to their hearts during the fall holy days.

> "You shall tithe all the yield of your seed that comes from the field year by year. And before the LORD your God, in the place that he will choose, to make his name dwell there, you shall eat the tithe of your grain, of your wine, and of your oil, and the firstborn of your herd and flock, that you may learn to fear the LORD your God always. And if the way is too long for you, so that you are not able to carry the tithe, when the LORD your God blesses you, because the place is too far from you, which the LORD your God chooses, to set his name there, then you shall turn it into money and bind up the money in your hand and go to the place that the LORD your God chooses and spend the money for whatever you desire— oxen or sheep or wine or strong drink, whatever your appetite craves. And you shall eat there before the LORD your God and rejoice, you and your household. (Deuteronomy 14:22-26)

Though one purpose of these visits to Jerusalem was spiritual observance, one gets the impression that the Lord also recognized their need for vacations, and even commanded them to maintain a vacation fund for that purpose.

I have found vacation time to be a necessity, and I would encourage you to include it in your strategy. At times when my job was especially demanding, I found that I needed the first week of vacation just to unwind and a second week to actually re-create.

In making decisions as CEO of our lives related to caring for ourselves, it is important to identify and keep our focus on the underlying purpose. Though the Lord "richly provides us with everything to enjoy" (1 Timothy 6:17), the ultimate, long-range goal is not to have fun but to maximize agape. Enjoying ourselves represents a means to that end. We engage in re-creation to maintain and enhance our capacity for agape production. Confusing the means and the ends will result in the tail wagging the dog, our living for recreation instead of agape production, and consequently spending excessive time, money, and other resources for that purpose.

Eliminate Excessive Overhead

Maximizing profits requires eliminating excessive overhead. A CEO might like the idea of a company jet and a nice new facility that includes large offices overlooking fountains. However, unless he can show how these amenities produce sufficient profits to justify their cost, they represent unnecessary overhead that will erode the bottom line. A good CEO will seek to identify and eliminate such waste.

In her book, *Through Gates of Splendor*,[xiii] Elisabeth Elliot records that in the early days of missionary aviation it was crucial for planes to deliver the maximum possible payload to missionaries. Many living in primitive circumstances had an urgent need for medicines and other necessities. A missionary pilot noted that these airplanes came equipped with comfortable, cushioned seats that weighed 7 pounds. He replaced them with less comfortable ones weighing 1 pound. Six fewer pounds of comfortable overhead allowed them to deliver six additional pounds of agape to needy missionaries. Likewise, managing our personal lives for maximum agape production requires that we redirect resources used for excessive overhead toward agape producing objectives.

A danger for contemporary Americans resides in allowing our culture to determine our needs. It is not so much that we are trying to keep up with our neighbors, though that may be a factor, but rather that we are allowing cultural norms to dictate "needs." Not that many years ago, most American homes were quite simple: a living room, dining room, kitchen, one bathroom, and enough bedrooms to accommodate everyone, which included packing some with a couple of kids. People survived quite well with this arrangement, and a healthy byproduct may have been learning to share. I am not suggesting this as a model but only mention it to make the point that many of the things our society now views as necessities really are not.

Those "needs" often require the support of two incomes, which leads to the need for daycare, perhaps an additional vehicle, added clothing, eating out more frequently or purchasing more prepared meals, paying more taxes, and other expenses. In other words, overhead begets overhead.

Let me accentuate that I am not suggesting what anyone should or should not have. Long ago I learned not to be judgmental about these things. A business person might purchase a $10 million yacht and use it as a means of closing a $20 million deal. For him the $10 million yacht was a great stewardship move that could produce maximum agape if he uses the profits for that purpose. Developing a comprehensive strategy and distributing resources to implement that strategy leads individuals to substantially different choices. A larger home may be a great investment that in the long run turns a substantial profit. A home in a more expensive area with better schools may represent an important agape investment in our children.

My point here is that as CEO of our lives we must eliminate unproductive overhead in order to produce maximum agape. That should be our ultimate objective. We must keep in mind that all the company resources belong to the Lord. Consequently, unnecessary overhead represents a misuse of the Lord's assets.

To avoid misunderstanding of what I am saying, I want to refer back to the previous section on killing the goose that lays the golden egg. Caring for personal needs, and those of our family, even ones like recreation, does not represent extravagance. We can be extravagant in these areas if we do not manage them well, but these areas of personal care per se represent genuine needs.

A less tangible but equally as important consideration has to do with aesthetics. God has designed us to enjoy beauty of all kinds. Usually beauty comes at a price. A drab apartment with orange crates for furniture might be functional, but it would also be depressing. Because of our aesthetic sensibilities, paying extra for pleasant surroundings does not comprise unnecessary overhead. Obviously, the "how much" question comes into play here. "My artistic sensibilities can only be satisfied with original Monet paintings" may represent an exaggerated estimation of what constitutes genuine needs. Needless to say, meeting aesthetic needs comprises a very subjective realm in which each of us must make his or her own decisions and do so thoughtfully. It is easy for one person to pamper himself in his estimation of his aesthetic needs and another to consign himself to an unpainted concrete existence. How good that we have the Holy Spirit to help us in the decision-making process.

The factors described above deal with optimal resource distribution. However, optimal resource distribution requires that we must maintain control of our resources. The next chapter addresses the challenges of achieving that objective.

Principle #10
Maintain Control of Your Resources

The ABC Widget Company was in trouble, having lost money for four of the past five years under Oscar's management. The board hired Joe to restore ABC's profits. A major challenge confronting Joe, perhaps a major reason for the company's decline under Oscar, resided in people seeking control of company resources to advance their own agendas, a source of profit erosion. Once Joe got settled into his new job, these people began to make their appearances.

One board member, not representing the board as a whole but promoting his personal agenda, paid a visit to Joe to relate that the company's visibility in the community had been substantially enhanced by its significant annual donation to the local women's shelter. His wife happened to chair this charity's board. He pressured Joe to continue this "company tradition" established by the previous CEO, adding a subtle threat that failing to do so would convey to the community that he did not care about women. Joe certainly did not want to alienate a board member or appear to be misogynist, but he also realized that the company needed this money to repair aging equipment.

Ralph, the softball coach, continued his efforts to get the team released an hour early on Tuesdays and Thursdays, emphasizing the significant boost a winning team gave to employee morale. Joe certainly wanted to be supportive of the team and see their winning record continue. However, he calculated that when the team left work early it became difficult for the other employees to do their jobs effectively, thus slowing overall production. In addition, he wondered how the other employees felt about the team getting time off to play ball while they continued at the daily grind. Though the coach made the participation of these players seem like an altruistic sacrifice for the company, Joe sensed that they were primarily motivated by their love for playing softball. In essence, the coach wanted to grab hold of a couple of hours of company resources, which Joe felt that the company could not spare at this time.

The next morning Joe received a call from Bill Stevens, CEO of GrassRoots, a local lawn care company. He informed Joe that the previous CEO played 18 holes of golf with him and two other local businessmen two afternoons a week and expressed hope that Joe would continue this practice. In this instance, the force seeking to take control of company resources was Joe's own desires. He loved to play golf, was quite good at it, and enjoyed the social interaction as well. He also knew that the business connections he made on the golf course could be advantageous. However, he realized that at this time in the company's history it needed his full-time attention to stop the bleeding and start making a profit again. Besides, if he took time off to play golf a couple of afternoons each week, he would be hard-pressed to deny the softball team one hour on Tuesdays and Thursdays. He could play the CEO card with them, but that would probably make matters worse. He had to exercise discipline over his own cravings for golf in order to maintain the best use of company resources for profit-making.

These represented just three of a dozen situations Joe encountered that would take company resources out of company control and away from profit production. He struggled with what to do. In the first two instances he did not want the animosity that would result from his negative responses, and in the third instance he did not want to deny himself of an activity he enjoyed. Yet, he concluded that it was just this sort of loss of control of company resources, and the company culture it engendered, that resulted in the previous CEO losing money. He decided that turning the company around required that he maintain control of company resources and manage the fallout resulting from turning down these requests.

Keeping Control of Resources

In the previous chapters we discussed the effective distribution of our resources. One challenge in pursuing that objective resides in maintaining control of the resources with which God has entrusted us.

God has placed resources under our authority. However, forces are seeking to move them out from under our control and place them under their own. Successful functioning as CEO of our lives requires that we resist these efforts and maintain control of our resources so that we can invest them most effectively. The discussion below identifies just a few of those forces.

People

Being a people pleaser might seem to be an expression of agape, but it is not. Often when we seek to please people we are not helping them. In fact, people pleasing actually comprises a form of selfishness. In essence it is saying, "I want you to like me so I will allow you to control my resources of time, effort, money, or whatever else it takes to gain your favor." In other words, *agape seeks the benefit of others while people pleasing seeks the approval of others.* These objectives are far from being the same.

Sometimes people pleasing takes the form of ministry. Scripture tells us that Jesus did not come to be served, but to serve. Therefore, all ministry to others seems to be reflecting the priorities of Jesus. I want to serve Jane, and she is having a crisis for the third day in a row. It seems that spending time with her to help her through her emotional struggles is what Jesus would do. Under this arrangement, Jane is actually controlling your resource of time and, depending on the circumstances, may be controlling much more.

As we examine the ministry of Jesus in Scripture we find that though He came to serve, He always served *on His terms.* He decided how and when He would use the resources His Father entrusted to Him. For example, in Luke 4:42-43 we read:

> And when it was day, he departed and went into a desolate place. And the people sought him and came to him, and would have kept him from leaving them, but he said to them, "I must preach the good news of the kingdom of God to the other towns as well; for I was sent for this purpose."

Jesus did not allow the people of Capernaum to control His resources but rather kept them under His own control so that He could use them as His Father directed, i.e. to produce maximum agape. That decision led Him to go a different direction than they had chosen for Him.

It is easy to see how allowing others to control our resources relates to codependency. In effect, enablers may view themselves as displaying agape, but they are really allowing the person they are enabling to use their agape-producing resources for counterproductive ends.

People seek to gain control of our resources in other ways also such as intimidation. Though others may not consciously seek to intimidate us or may not even be aware that they are, nonetheless their dominant personalities may exert a degree of control over our decisions, inclining us toward bad choices we otherwise would not make. The board member seeking a contribution to the women's shelter may possess a dominant personality, a factor that could influence Joe to make a bad decision.

Desires

Another force, perhaps the dominant one, that causes us to turn over control of our resources resides in our own desires. Those desires come in a variety of forms such as addictions, love of recreation and entertainment, cravings for attention and popularity, romantic and sexual desires, and an inordinate desire for relaxation. We have already noted that a legitimate place exists for recreation and other factors related to our own well-being, but it is essential that we do not allow our desires to move our choices beyond that legitimate boundary.

Joe desperately wanted to play golf, but he realized that his time was one of the company's most valuable assets and that turning two afternoons each week over to that desire would not only squander that resource but would set a negative example.

Capitulating control in one area seems not only to affect that aspect of our lives but also erodes our discipline in general. For example, if we yield control to our appetite for food, we find ourselves less likely to exercise, more likely to stay up late, and more inclined to lose control of our resources in general.

Calculated Consignment of Control

We have been discussing the danger of losing control of the resources at our disposal. However, frequently we find ourselves in situations where it is beneficial to consign control of certain resources to others in exchange for benefits.

Maintaining citizenship in the United States requires consigning certain freedoms and resources to the government. We must obey the laws and pay taxes. However, we receive many benefits in return. It would be virtually impossible to live without allegiance to some nation, and most of us conclude that we are blessed by the opportunity to align ourselves with the United States of America. Likewise, taking out a mortgage for our home gives the bank a degree of control over our lives, but it also provides us with the many benefits of home ownership.

Marriage requires a major consignment of control but the returns are substantial. The same is true of parenting, employment, church affiliation, and other commitments.

In the context of functioning as CEO of our lives, these commitments need to be weighed against their capacity to enhance agape production. While it may sound rather calculating to frame a commitment to marriage in those terms, this perspective actually may provide a beneficial way to look at marriage and enable the person contemplating marriage to avoid mistakes. We might ask, will this relationship produce substantial agape in the life of my future spouse? Am I marrying this person just for selfish reasons without considering the impact on her or him? Are we sufficiently compatible that together we will engender an agape-producing environment for children and comprise a good team for benefiting others? Are our objectives sufficiently compatible that we will be pulling together, thus allowing us to optimize the production of agape?

These considerations are especially important as related to marriage because that commitment is, or at least should be, irreversible, profound, and all-encompassing. However, we might ask similar questions in regard to all decisions that consign control of our resources to some other person or entity. Mistakes in doing so carry a high cost. On the other hand, these types of relationships when established thoughtfully can enable us to produce significantly more agape.

The previous chapters have discussed various factors related to making good management decisions. However, success as CEO of our lives requires that we effectively manage ourselves. The chapter ahead discusses major factors related to achieving that objective.

Principle #11
Manage Yourself

As Joe wrapped up his second quarter at ABC Widget Company, he had good reason to be encouraged. R&D had come up with some good ideas for new products, the equipment was now in good shape and being maintained, employee morale was high, sales were up slightly, and the board seemed satisfied with Joe's work.

Though Joe felt confident that he was managing the company well, he began to wonder whether his focus on the company had not resulted in allowing management of his personal life to slip. For years he had maintained a routine of swinging by Gold's Gym after work on Mondays, Wednesdays, and Fridays. One Wednesday, after facing some special challenges at work he decided to go straight home. Doing so was just too easy and comfortable. He did it again Friday. The weeks that followed found him making it to the gym only once or maybe twice a week, and some weeks not at all. He started to feel sluggish and gained five pounds. Next, his morning Bible reading and prayer time started to slip. He realized that this erosion of essential routines spelled trouble, and consequently he began work on reinstating them.

Self-Management

At one level, the theme of this entire book has been self-management. The essence of functioning as CEO of one's life entails managing every aspect of our existence for profitability. For example, we have discussed personal issues such as the need to care for our health. This chapter, however, deals with self-management issues closer to the core of our existence.

Overcoming Inertia and Maintaining Momentum

A major impediment to managing of our lives is inertia, the resistance to transition from a resting state to motion. In the world of physics, we discover that it requires a significant amount of energy to move from one state to another. For example, it necessitates considerable energy to take H_2O from a fluid to a gaseous state (steam). It only requires one calorie of energy to increase 1 gram of water by 1°C. So to increase its temperature from 0°C, right at freezing, to 100°C, right at boiling, only requires 100 calories. However, to transform that 1 gram of water at the boiling point into steam requires 540 calories. In other words, this phase change demands over five times more energy than is required to take that gram of water from freezing to boiling. You have heard that old adage, "A watched pot never boils." Now you know why. It takes a whole lot more energy to make it boil than just to make it hot.

Phase changes come hard. That is true of our personalities as well. The transition from the stationary phase to the movement phase demands a lot of energy. When I am relaxing on the couch, as the time approaches for me to get up to do some work, it almost feels as if a force is holding me down, making the challenge of getting up and doing something productive seem almost overwhelming. Once I exercise the totality of my willpower, overcome inertia, and get myself in motion, I am always amazed at how easy it is to do what seemed like an overwhelming task a few minutes earlier while I was being held captive by the couch.

I experience this same force exerting its influence almost every time I am required to overcome inertia. Some projects I dread doing. The longer I put them off, the more insurmountable they become. However, once I overcome inertia and start doing them, I actually enjoy the activity. Consequently, inertia comprises a major enemy of productivity.

At times we may lose the battle with it, allowing it to prevent us from achieving. When the time comes to exercise, how often have we allowed inertia to win? Allowing inertia to get the upper hand raises the danger of developing a pattern of capitulating to it. Every time it wins it gets stronger, making it easier to give into it the following time, and the time after that it is easier yet. On the other hand, each defeat of inertia reduces its power.

One strategy for overcoming inertia entails choosing easier tasks as a means of getting started. If I am relaxing, the thought of going to the gym can seem overwhelming. However, putting on my workout clothes is relatively easy. And once I begin that process, I have overcome inertia and gained some momentum, making heading toward the gym almost spontaneous. In other words, we can overcome inertia by not focusing on the whole journey but only on the first step.

That brings us to the topic of momentum. Once we take the first step, we have developed a degree of momentum which carries us to future steps and ultimately to the completion of the project. An old cliché instructs us, "If you want something done, ask a busy person to do it." This is the case because the busy person has overcome inertia and has developed a full head of momentum, which enables him or her to take new challenges in stride.

Overcoming inertia and gaining and maintaining

momentum constitutes a major factor in successfully managing ourselves. Many people fall short of maximum agape production because they have developed a habit of capitulating to inertia, consequently failing to develop and maintain momentum. Successful people have come to realize that inertia is lying to them when it conveys that getting started is too hard. They realize that once they begin and develop some momentum, the work will actually be enjoyable and fulfilling. That realization provides them with the motivation to win the battle against inertia and live a life full of momentum, which in turn not only leads to substantial productivity but also makes the journey enjoyable.

Goals

One means of overcoming inertia and maintaining momentum resides in goal setting. Goals give us the incentive to overcome inertia. If I merely think it would be a good idea to go to the gym, I might easily convince myself that a person in my condition should not be lifting all those weights. However, if I have established a goal of going to the gym every Monday through Friday at 7:30 pm, and it is Thursday and I have made it every day this week so far, this goal motivates me to break the grip of the couch monster and start putting on my workout clothes. Likewise, leaving the time for completion of a job open-ended encourages a casual pace whereas identifying the finish line prompts a more aggressive approach.

Like strategy in general, goals need to be updated as situations change. Unrealistic goals can become counterproductive, serving as brutal taskmasters that push us beyond healthy limits, robbing other aspects of our life of their legitimate place and sapping life of its joy. It is essential to choose goals wisely.

Energy

Possessing a personality that exudes energy elevates our agape-producing capabilities. People seek to borrow energy from others, and therefore they are attracted to those who project it. Virtually every successful entertainer projects a high energy level. That is one reason we are drawn to them. As we observe them closely we recognize that their voice, face, and body language are all exuding energy. The same applies to us. If we project energy, we will have greater influence with others.

Scripture instructs us to approach life passionately. In Ecclesiastes 9:10, Solomon charges: "Whatever your hand finds to do, do it with your might." Likewise, the apostle Paul in Colossians 3:23 instructs, "Whatever you do, work heartily, as for the Lord and not for men." Imagine if Jesus asked you to set up chairs for a service at church, and He stood there watching you work. Most of us would do the most aggressive and proficient job of setting up chairs ever. Paul is telling us that we should approach every task with that same energy, realizing that Jesus in fact is watching.

Doing so is most effectively achieved not by drumming up energy artificially but by being genuinely passionate about life in general and about displaying agape toward others in particular. Being passionate about life is a product of our perspective. Thinking negatively regarding the tasks before us will sap our energy, leaving us depleted before we start. If instead, we follow the instruction of Paul cited above and do everything as an assignment from the Lord and in service to Him, this perspective will boost our energy level. In addition, reflecting on the benefits that our actions will bring others will heighten our energy level.

As we have already discussed, all our activities should be calculated to display agape in some form ("Let all that you do be done in love"), whether it is giving someone a smile or doing a great job at work. Consequently, all that we do should convey enthusiasm, knowing that doing so will benefit others.

A major fringe benefit of exuding energy resides in the momentum it produces in our own lives, which will enable us to work at the highest level of productivity, overcome obstacles, take challenges in stride, prevent lethargy, and ward off fear and other negative emotions. One is hard-pressed to find a successful person who does not exude a high level of energy.

Routine

The Benefits of Routine

The Mir Space Station utilizes 11 gyroscopes to keep it oriented toward the sun.[xiv] Routines comprise the gyroscopes of our personal life. Good habits keep us oriented in a healthy, productive direction. If we would approach every day as if we were in a whole new world in which we must make choices from scratch, we would quickly become disoriented. If, however, we wake up to a set of routines that we have discovered will promote a productive lifestyle, our chance of success increases substantially.

Routine helps in two ways. First, it prompts us to practice behaviors that we have discovered to be successful. Of course, a routine consisting of bad practices leads to failure. A habit of consuming a half-gallon of rocky road prior to bedtime invites major trouble. However, as we incorporate into our schedule practices that have proven to enhance our physical, emotional, relational, and spiritual health, we optimize our lives.

In addition, routine helps us overcome the inertia of life, instead enabling us to maintain momentum. We just discussed the power and dangers of inertia. Therefore, any help in overcoming it is valuable. Routines enable us to defeat it and gain momentum because we tend to follow them almost spontaneously. If a person routinely goes to the gym on his way home from work, after a while he finds that the car almost drives itself there. Getting out, going into the locker room, putting on workout clothes, and beginning to exercise are practically spontaneous.

Some Essential Routines

We have already alluded to several habits that promote maximum agape production. Meaningful Bible study would come at the top of that list. We have also noted the significance of prayer. To be effective, prayer requires substantial time and needs to be achieved in a venue and manner in which we can focus on our conversation with the Lord. People have told me, "I pray all the time," which I suspect means that they do not devote any particular time to prayer. Though praying throughout the day, talking with our partner, the Holy Spirit, is a valuable practice, if Jesus needed a time of concentrated prayer alone with His Father, it is certain that we do also.

Most people find that they can only develop a meaningful routine of Bible study and prayer if they assign the first part of the day for that purpose. Once the day gets started, our mind is too cluttered to focus on those practices, and we tend to keep putting them off until the day has ended and we have once again failed to engage in them. We can avoid this result by devoting the beginning of the day to them.

Starting the day with Bible study and prayer also gets our day off on the right foot, orienting us toward spiritual values and agape production. In addition, beginning the day with these disciplines gives us momentum for achieving the tasks ahead.

Scripture indicates that an effective connection with a body of believers should also be habitual. God has not designed us to go it alone. We need one another. Scripture describes us as a body. We need the blood supply and other commodities provided by the body. Spiritual health requires it. Those lacking this meaningful connection are placing themselves at great risk and are stunting their spiritual growth.

Most people need a good exercise regimen to maintain their health. It is also beneficial to develop the habit of a healthy bedtime. It can be helpful to set the alarm on your smartphone to get you moving in that direction at the appropriate time.

It is also beneficial to establish a pattern for eating that in general includes what, how much, and when you eat. Our selection of foods differs from day to day, but we can decide on basic types of foods and the amounts that we eat at given times. For example, at supper we might choose to limit our food intake to one serving and decide on the basic size of that portion. We might decide to eat dessert only after supper, and then restrict that to a moderate portion. One advantage to developing this type of eating pattern is that once we have established it, we can make moderate adjustments as needed.

Likewise, establishing routines in all areas can be helpful. If we do not have a routine for relaxation, it is easy for life to become drudgery. Routines for everything from mowing the grass to paying our bills can help keep our lives organized and orderly. I have discovered that when an area of my life gets out of control, the cause is often an absence of routine in that area. Formulating a practice that addresses that issue brings it under control.

If we allow routines to become our masters, they can have a negative effect. It is important that we analyze them to determine whether they are making positive contributions to our life or whether some modification is necessary.

Routine tends to produce and maintain order to our lives, enabling us to combat the chaos that is constantly seeking to force its way into our existence. The more good habits we establish, the more likely that our lives will be kept on course by the gyroscopes they provide.

Honoring Our Commitments to Ourselves

We can create and maintain the lifestyle structures described above by making thoughtful commitments to ourselves regarding best practices. Making a commitment to ourselves must not be done lightly or impulsively. Rather, it should be done thoughtfully and prayerfully. Such commitments should not be like New Year's resolutions, most of which are forgotten long before February or even before January 2. Rather, they should be the result of serious, prayerful analysis and only after we have counted the cost.

It is wise never to make more than one commitment at a time, and then only to commit ourselves to small changes. For someone who has not been jogging, committing himself to run 5 miles per day is a bad idea. I can guarantee that he will not stay with it for more than a week. Or if a person who has not regulated his diet decides on a stringent program, he will probably not succeed for long. Small, well-thought-out alterations represent wise commitments.

Having committed ourselves, it is important that we not break those commitments. Most commitments should be made with the understanding that only emergencies or changing situations warrant altering the program. Apart from such contingencies, however, it is essential that we maintain the commitments we have made to ourselves. Getting into the habit of lying to ourselves, of making and then breaking commitments to ourselves, or making illegitimate exceptions, will result in a weak character and a chaotic life.

This prescription for maintaining a structured life eliminates impulsivity. For the most part, impulsivity and effective management do not mix. We should not be impulsive in making commitments, in breaking commitments, or for that matter in anything else that we do. Almost any decision made on impulse, any commitment, any purchase, any statement ("you are just like your mother"), any change in plans, virtually any impulsive behavior at all that is not in response to an emergency, will almost invariably result in loss and remorse. Rather than promote agape production, you will almost certainly obstruct it. By way of contrast, carefully formulating commitments to ourselves and a regular practice of honoring those commitments engenders both a strong character and an organized lifestyle that produces substantial agape.

Using Negative Circumstances as a Springboard for Future Success

At the outset of this book I described regrets that I have experienced due to past failures. Those regrets left me with two options. I could either wallow in them or use them to motivate me to benefit others. I mentioned that my prime motive in writing this book was to help others avoid my mistakes. Wasted years have also motivate me to make full use of the ones I still have.

We can translate virtually every negative experience into motivation for achieving good, i.e. producing agape. I had a friend who while receiving treatment for cancer would go around the facility praying with and seeking to cheer up other patients. Her own diagnosis gave her a special connection with them that made her ministry meaningful. She used her negative experience as a motivation to display agape.

My father-in-law, who was a pastor for many years, lost a daughter who was only several months old. Throughout his ministry he used this tragedy to provide a special connection with people who had experienced a loss. Often they would respond, "You understand, don't you pastor?"

Losing a job can motivate us to retool and find a better one. Failing at a task can make us all the more determined to do better next time and to pursue the means of making that happen. The apostle Paul instructed in Romans 12:21, "Do not be overcome by evil, but overcome evil with good." Every failure, every setback, every loss, has inherent within it an opportunity to turn it around for good. We succeed at life by discovering and using those opportunities.

The Replacement Principle

We have been discussing the use of negative circumstances as a motivation for achieving good. A related but somewhat different principle resides in combating negative qualities in our lives by replacing them with positive ones. It is difficult if not impossible to just stop negative habits because doing so leaves a void, and in time the old habits tend to return with a vengeance.

Jesus told the story of an unclean spirit who had left a man, but later returning found "the house empty, swept, and put in order." In response, he moved back in, taking seven of his demon buddies with him, leaving the man far worse off. Ultimately a vacuum will be filled, and if we do not intentionally fill it with something positive, we can be sure that a negative force will move in. Remember, chaos is the default setting.

Consequently, successfully overcoming bad habits and other negative aspects of our lives requires replacing the negative with something positive. Paul demonstrates this principle in Ephesians 4:28: "Let the thief no longer steal, but rather let him labor, doing honest work with his own hands, so that he may have something to share with anyone in need." He instructs the thief to replace stealing with working and giving. In fact, in that chapter Paul gives many applications of this replacement principle. For example:

> Let all bitterness and wrath and anger and clamor and slander be put away from you, along with all malice. Be kind to one another, tenderhearted, forgiving one another, as God in Christ forgave you. (Ephesians 4:31-32)

We do not stop nasty behaviors by sitting on our hands but by replacing them with kindness. We might replace overeating with exercise or viewing unwholesome movies or television programming with learning a new, productive skill to fill that time slot.

Subordinate Gratification to Achievement

Success requires achievement—getting things done. Perhaps the greatest enemy of achievement is a focus on gratification. If our thoughts, interests, and values revolve around eating, entertainment, sex, or some other form of gratification, the pursuit of them will become our primary focus, leaving achievement as a secondary objective. This priority structure will result in our failure to live up to our potential. When my next meal or my next snack becomes my focus, and work becomes a necessary evil sandwiched in between food intake, I will produce at a low level.

Of course, all of the desires listed above are natural and good when subordinated to the pursuit of achievement. But when some sort of gratification constitutes our primary interest, it distorts our decision-making and distracts from our productivity.

It seems that some people are achievement-oriented by nature while others are more focused on gratification. However, virtually all people have some area in their lives in which gratification supersedes achievement—in the words of the author of Hebrews, "the sin that so easily besets," which goes unnamed because it differs for each of us. Julius Caesar was one of history's most achievement-oriented people. Yet, after developing a relationship with Cleopatra, he spent valuable time cruising up the Nile with her while virtually every corner of the Roman Empire was descending into chaos. Whatever form gratification may take, if given priority it will distort decision-making and attenuate productivity.

Jesus modeled assigning priority to achievement when He refused to eat in anticipation of the arrival of the men of Sychar. He explained to His disciples, "My food is to do the will of him who sent me and to accomplish his work." (John 4:34)

In addition to curtailing productivity, placing priority on gratification almost invariably results in it, like a cancerous growth, occupying a disproportionate place in our lives, forcing legitimate pursuits out of their appropriate space. And like a cancerous growth, it will invariably produce some type of physical, behavioral, emotional, or relational pathology in our lives. For example, an exaggerated preoccupation with entertainment can displace sleep, exercise, spiritual practices, and even the demands of work, which will ultimately lead to physiological, relational, financial, and other types of problems.

Resolving this problem requires the appropriation of the power of the Holy Spirit. Also helpful is a shift of the focus of our thought-life away from gratification and toward achievement. If we focus our thoughts on and engage in agape-producing activities we will discover that they are far more rewarding than self-gratification. This joy of agape-production will provide the motivation needed to shift our priorities from gratification to achievement.

Make Prime Use of Primetime

From 8 o'clock to 11:00 PM comprises primetime for television, the hours when viewership promises to be the greatest. The biggest names get those cherished times, and advertisers pay more for them.

Likewise, we all have primetime for productivity, those hours when our mind is clearest, our energy level is highest, and we are relatively free from distractions. Managing for optimal output requires that we identify and make the best use of those times, using them to do our most significant and creative work. We can do routine tasks fairly effectively at other times. When I am writing, the creation of new material requires primetime hours. I can edit existing material at other times.

Conversely, good management calls us to use those times when our bodies and brains are depleted for relaxation. Not only is our capacity to produce at its lowest during those times but our capacity to relax is the greatest. When I have tried to use those hours to be productive, usually the end product has been bad. The time was wasted, and I felt frustrated that I did not use that time to get the relaxation I desperately needed.

Therefore, good management requires that we identify primetime, routine time, and downtime, and use each category to the best advantage. We can also enhance productivity by finding ways to increase primetime and routine time and minimize downtime to reasonable limits.

I have also discovered that I can take more constructive approaches to downtime. For example, I find reading biographies instead of novels can be relaxing and yet educational. Listening to books rather than music can also be more productive. Please do not misunderstand. I am not asserting that there is no time for novels and music, but I am saying that managing our downtime wisely can provide us with refreshment as well as other benefits. In this regard, I return to our uniqueness, which requires that every person identify his or her own optimal approach to downtime.

Bring Dead Time to Life

Early in my marriage I realized that my wife, Connie, was far more productive than I was. No doubt numerous factors contributed to that, but I identified one that has been especially helpful. Whenever I had large blocks of time, I would use them to get things done. However, I viewed the cracks between those blocks as downtime, occasions when I could put my feet up on my desk and put my mind in neutral. I figured that I could not get much done in those short periods, and therefore I might as well just relax.

I noticed, however, that Connie seized those moments to accomplish a variety of tasks. As I observed, I was amazed at how much she could get done during those in between times. As I began to follow her example, I became far more productive.

I noticed that not only was I able to use those stray minutes to check items off my to-do list, but also doing so enabled me to maintain the momentum that carried me into the next major task. My old approach to life entailed starting, stopping, and starting again, resulting in constantly losing momentum and therefore consequently needing to overcome inertia all over again. That approach to life demanded far more energy, and accomplished far less, than maintaining ongoing momentum. I was not only getting less done but having to work harder to achieve what I did accomplish..

All the principles for succeeding as CEO of our lives already described are rooted in one final concept that is identified in the chapter ahead.

Principle #12
Commit Yourself

As Joe reflected back over the previous twelve months, he was gratified by how his work as CEO had transformed ABC Widget Company. Compared with its condition when he took over, the company was hardly recognizable, being in a significantly better state in every area. Its financial condition was sound, its products had been updated, its equipment was now well maintained, sales had increased substantially, and esprit among personnel was high. As he pondered what had precipitated this transformation, he traced its roots to two related factors.

This remaking of the company began when he committed himself to assume the authority and the related responsibility as CEO. The board did not extend to him the option of coming in for a few hours a week to try out functioning as CEO to see how he liked it and whether it was a good fit. In retrospect, he realized that this approach is virtually never tried because it could not work. The employees would not have viewed him or responded to him as CEO because he had not made the commitment necessary to fill that position. He would not have had the authority to make decisions or spend money or make meaningful changes. No partial arrangement was possible. Becoming CEO of ABC Widget Company had to be like diving off a diving board. The options were limited to not diving or diving. It had to begin with a total commitment made at a point in time.

The board made him an offer and asked him to make a decision by the following Friday. He had thought about that commitment, prayed about it, and discussed it with his wife and a few trusted friends. Then the day came. Joe opted to commit to the position of CEO of ABC Widget Company. Since Joe was a man of his word, perhaps that commitment came at the point where he announced to the board, "Thank you for your offer. I have decided to accept it." Legally it came a few minutes later when he signed the agreement.

Joe realized that the radical makeover now in evidence all around him required that he or someone with his capabilities make that commitment. Any path to its transformation had to start there.

Many factors had prepared Joe for that moment of commitment. Good training by his parents provided a solid foundation. His schoolwork, including his BA in business administration and MBA, gave him the essential knowledge. He then received valuable experience in subordinate management positions, both through his own work and observing the management styles of his supervisors. The sum total of these experiences had qualified him to assume the role of CEO and to make the related commitment.

Joe also realized, however, that his commitment, though comprising an essential first step, by itself was not sufficient to produce that transformation. That commitment necessarily had to lead to a mindset that would translate commitment into profit. He had to start thinking in terms of using his new authority to meet the commensurate responsibilities. His thoughts, at least during his working hours, had to be occupied with identifying the most effective means of using company resources to produce maximum profit. Furthermore, he had to be thinking about how to transform those ideas into achievement. In other words, Joe recognized that his thought-life served as the bridge that would take him from commitment to success.

The Call to Commitment

Serious change must begin with a commitment. The apostle Paul in Romans 12:1 says, "I appeal to you therefore, brothers, by the mercies of God, to present your bodies as a living sacrifice, holy and acceptable to God, which is your spiritual worship." The phrase "present your bodies" comprises a call to commitment.

Paul is not making a salvation appeal in this passage since he is addressing "brothers," that is, believers. In fact, the book is written to believers—the church in Rome. The preceding chapters have all been written from the perspective that his readers are believers.

Why this call to believers to make a commitment? What is the nature of the commitment Paul has in view? We have been talking about management throughout this book. God has directed us to manage our lives to maximize agape production. We have mentioned that under the New Covenant we are executives in God's family business. Management, making executive decisions, requires maturity. Children or even adolescents cannot make those kinds of decisions. General Electric will not be hiring a teenage CEO any time soon.

This is true of baby believers as well. New Christians need to be discipled so that they can develop in their understanding of the Christian life and apply that knowledge to their lifestyle. As we mature in our knowledge and the applications of the teaching of Scripture, we arrive at the point where we are ready to assume the responsibilities related to functioning as CEO of our lives.

Having reached that point, as with Joe when he took on the position of CEO of ABC Widget Company, we need to commit ourselves to the responsibilities related to functioning as CEO of our lives. It is that commitment to which Paul is calling believers in Romans 12:1. Specifically, Paul is calling us to commit ourselves to manage our lives to maximize agape output. He specifically exhorts us to present our bodies. He does so because our bodies, i.e. our brains, our hands, our feet, our ears, our mouth, and other physical assets, provide the channels for conveying agape.

This commitment requires the presentation of our bodies as a living sacrifice. Sacrifice conveys death. A commitment to agape production entails dying to a lifestyle that places us at the center of our universe. We present ourselves as a living sacrifice in that having died to selfishness we are to live to benefit God and others.

The Need for Commitment

The first 11 chapters of the book of Romans makes clear that we are already obligated to live for the Lord. Christ died for our redemption, and therefore we are obligated to live for him. In 2 Corinthians 5:15 Paul frames our obligation in these terms, "(A)nd He died for all, that those who live should live no longer for themselves, but for Him who died for them and rose again." (NKJV) In Romans 12:1, Paul expresses this obligation by referring to this commitment as our "reasonable service." The Greek word for "reasonable" is related to the English word logical and the practice of accounting. In essence Paul is saying that as we assess the debits and credits related to what Christ has done for us, it is only reasonable that we should employ our lives in service for Him.

Since Paul has already established this obligation, why the need for commitment? Instead, why does Paul not adopt the Nike slogan, "Just do it"? The passage that follows includes numerous instructions related to living a life characterized by agape. Why is it not sufficient for him to just tell us how to live and then turn us loose to follow those instructions? Why does he instead begin this application section of Romans by calling us to commit ourselves to that lifestyle?

In short, commitment constitutes a significant first step in producing change. This passage is about change—transformation. As human beings, change comes hard. This reality is evidenced by the huge size of the change industry in our society. Diet programs, health clubs, therapy, and more recently life coaches represent just a few aspects of our society designed to help us change.

Because making changes is so difficult for human beings, meaningful change necessarily begins with commitment. Virtually every significant change in life is preceded by a commitment. Marriage is. The commitment embodied in the vows comprises the essence of the wedding ceremony. Our society currently is trying an approach to "marriage" that does not require commitment, i.e. cohabitation. Statistics related to this trend indicate that it is not working well for couples, their children, or society as a whole. A relationship as profound as marriage requires that it be launched with a commitment. A person entering the military takes an oath, as does one assuming a major government position. The same is true of those becoming citizens.

Why is commitment foundational to change? Simply because it acknowledges our moral responsibility to live a certain way, to practice certain behaviors. That acknowledgment, in turn, provides motivation to practice those behaviors.

Just as it was necessary for Joe to make a commitment to the board, a commitment to the Lord to meet the responsibilities of CEO of our lives provides the incentive we need to function successfully. If we employ the slogan, "Just do it" in adopting a lifestyle characterized by agape, on the days when we tend not to feel like just doing it, it is all too easy to just not do it. However, our commitment to God provides the necessary inducement to rise above selfish inclinations, even when displaying agape is difficult.

I would urge you to prayerfully consider pausing now and making a commitment to the Lord to fulfill the role He has assigned you as CEO of your life, accepting the responsibility from this point forward to use your resources to produce maximum agape for Him. At times when you are confronted with powerful incentives to slip back into a selfish orientation, reflecting on that commitment will provide a strong motivation to continue managing your life for maximum agape production.

Our Thought-Life

As Joe noted, though essential, commitment is not enough. We must follow through on commitment by adopting a mindset that transforms commitment into profit. The apostle Paul made this point in Romans 12:2. Immediately after his call to commitment, he instructed his reader, "be transformed by the renewal of your mind."

The Greek word for "transform" used in this passage is the same term used to describe the transfiguration of Christ. It is the Greek term from which we derive the English "metamorphosis." It literally means to change form. Just as the metamorphosis process transforms the not so pretty caterpillar into a beautiful butterfly, our thoughts possess that same power to transform our lives from their not so attractive self-centered form into beautiful other-centered beings.

So there you have it. That sounds easy enough. Just maintain agape-oriented thoughts, and you will be transformed into an agape-producing person. Unfortunately, doing so is not so easy. To help us grasp why, we might think of our mind in terms of a computer.

The computer of your mind has two primary programs loaded on it. The apostle Paul describes this dual mindset and the significance of accessing the correct one in Romans 8:6: "For the mind set on the flesh is death, but the mind set on the Spirit is life and peace." This translation, which is accurate, indicates that we have two minds.

We might describe one of those minds in terms of a computer program named Me-Maps. This program, loaded in our minds when we were born, maps out life with "me" at the center. Consequently, this program determines all our values based on promoting ourselves and our agenda. Me-Maps, however, provides us with an erroneous picture of life, and whenever we follow it we find ourselves getting lost. Me-Maps also creates relational problems because when married couples realize that they are lost, wives plead with their husbands to stop to get directions, but husbands, confident that Me-Maps is giving good information, just keep driving, resulting in even greater confusion and the obligatory "I told you so." Now they are lost and fighting.

When we received Christ and experienced the new birth, the Holy Spirit loaded a new program, You-Maps, in our mind, which maps out life accurately, with God at the center and others as significant attractions. If followed, You-Maps will get us to our desired destination, with couples happily chatting away on the trip.

As we study Scripture and grow in our relationship with the Lord, our new You-Maps program gets updated with version 1.1 and then 1.2 and ultimately service pack one and service pack two. These updates help us to avoid traffic jams and provide even better routes for getting us to our destination.

A major difficulty results because the Me-Maps program not only remains on the hard drive of our minds after we receive Christ but also on our Random Access Memory along with You-Maps, making both immediately accessible with a mouse click.

Our thoughts, what is appearing on the monitor of our mind, reflect which program we are accessing at any given moment. *The challenge confronting believers is not so much what we think about but which mind we are thinking with.* Are we accessing Me-Maps or You-Maps?

Which program we are accessing constitutes the most crucial aspect of our existence because the one appearing on the monitor of our minds determines our view of life at that moment. Success as CEO of our lives requires that we consistently access You-Maps, which leads toward agape production.

Doing so is especially challenging for two reasons. First, our operating system has designated Me-Maps as our default program. If someone says something we find offensive, Me-Maps tends to pop up spontaneously with responses such as, "Who do you think you are to judge me," or "Buddy, you have a great big log in your own eye that needs attention before you start criticizing me." It requires intention and discipline to switch to You-Maps, which might prompt thoughts such as, "I wonder if he is having a bad day. Maybe I should pray for him." Or "Maybe what he is saying is true. I need to give that prayerful consideration." Those kinds of thoughts require that we manually click off Me-Maps and click on the You-Maps icon with our mouse. Often we find doing that very difficult

The need to keep clicking off Me-Maps becomes annoying, but no one has been able to find a way to correct this glitch in our operating system. Therefore, maintaining an agape focus requires that we continuously and intentionally remove Me-Maps from the monitor of our minds and access You-Maps. If we let our mind wander even briefly, Me-Maps again pops up on the monitor of our minds, shaping our perspective on life.

Maintaining the mind of the Spirit, a You-Maps outlook on life, is difficult not only because our operating system has designated Me-Maps as the default program, but also because Me-Maps is very seductive. In mapping out the route to happiness, it starts us out on appealing roads such as, "Do what feels good," "Get all you can for yourself," "Get even," and the very popular "Immediate gratification."

Some of these routes are very scenic at the outset, seducing us to keep accessing Me-Maps. Me-Maps also tempts us to take a lot of feel-good shortcuts such as "Pornography," "Cheating," and "Deception." However, in the long run not only do these shortcuts get us lost, but they take us to extremely unsavory destinations such as "Wasted years," "Destroyed relationships," "Tarnished reputation," "Guilt," and "Remorse."

The routes mapped out by You-Maps are quite different, often initially taking us on rough roads such as "Discipline," "Patience," "Humility," and "Sacrifice." You-Maps also guides us onto some very pleasant highways and streets such as "Fellowship," "Good relationships," and "Clear conscience." You-Maps serves us well because it assures us that we are not lost and keeps us on the best routes to genuine fulfillment and success.

Nonetheless, the seduction of the initial roads and promised pleasures offered by Me-Maps arouses a very strong inclination to keep accessing that program instead of using You-Maps.

To help us understand why Me-Maps gets us lost and You-Maps takes us to our destination, it is important to recognize the difference in the quality of the data on each. For example, Me-Maps erroneously tells us that happiness comes from getting while You-Maps informs us that we derive happiness from giving. Me-Maps misleads us by asserting that this world is all that there is and therefore should be the basis for our values while You-Maps provides directions based on the existence of a spiritual world that determines valid principles for living. You-Maps data include both scientific and spiritual truths that can be integrated into a unified worldview that corresponds to and works in the real world.

That said, however, we can have a well-developed biblical worldview loaded on our You-Maps program, but if we allow Me-Maps to dominate our thought-life, all those wonderful truths will have no influence over our decisions and behaviors. In other words, it is not our knowledge, but our thought-life that ultimately determines all of the significant aspects of our existence: our attitudes, values, priorities, decisions, and lifestyle.

As a result of a lot of Bible study and a realistic understanding of the material world, Sean had loaded a well-developed biblical worldview on You-Maps, which included great truths such as his responsibility to invest his resources to benefit others and that it is more blessed to give than to receive.

However, a car dealership that he passed every day on the way to work had a lime green Lamborghini on the front lot for the bargain basement price of $160,000. It was love at first sight. Sean, in his mid-30s, a still single and successful entrepreneur, quickly calculated that by cutting just a little into his normal giving to ministry he could afford this car.

Sean first spotted the Lamborghini on his way home. The

next morning as he did his Bible study he began reflecting on the Lamborghini and realized that buying it would not be a good management decision, i.e. would not be the most effective use of his resources for producing agape. However, across the next two weeks both going to and coming from work, every time he passed the car lot Me-Maps would pop up and he would look longingly at the Lamborghini with growing fondness. Though Sean was not consciously aware of it, he started to view the purchase of this Lamborghini predominantly using Me-Maps. Though You-Maps would have confirmed his previous conclusion that this purchase was not the most effective use of his finances, he was now accessing that program far less frequently. His thoughts, now being formed largely by Me-Maps, were shaping his values and priorities, and were about to control his decision-making. Me-Maps suggested that it would not hurt to at least stop and take a closer look. Of course, the salesman immediately saw the glint in Sean's eye and in three minutes had him out for a test drive. The rest is history.

The moral of the story is that though Sean possessed a great biblical worldview loaded on You-Maps, i.e. his knowledge was well-developed, it was his thought-life, the mind through which he was thinking, which became dominated by Me-Maps, that determined his decisions and behaviors.

Across time the program that we access most frequently will shape our interests, values, and priorities. Ultimately it will determine our actions and our success as CEO of our life. As Paul teaches, again using the same Greek word for transformation, "But we all, with unveiled face, beholding as in a mirror the glory of the Lord, are being transformed into the same image from glory to glory, just as from the Lord, the Spirit." (2 Corinthians 3:18 NASB) As we follow through with our commitment of our lives as a living sacrifice by maintaining a focus on the Lord, viewing the world through You-Maps, the mind of the Spirit, we will experience that transformation and succeed as CEO of our lives.

This book reveals that managing our lives for success requires work and discipline. Perhaps while we are in the midst of doing all that work and exercising that discipline we might wonder whether the benefits are sufficient to make it worth the effort. The upcoming final chapter reveals that it is.

The Optimized Life

As Joe sat at his desk reflecting on how far ABC Widget Company had come during his first year as CEO, he experienced a sense of deep satisfaction. In trying to analyze his feelings of fulfillment, he realized that numerous factors were contributing to this experience.

Of course, he sensed satisfaction over all he had achieved. The building and equipment were in good shape and well maintained, and he had developed a plan for gradually updating the machinery. R&D had developed a creative widget that included a computer chip, enabling it to be voice controlled, a product none of his competitors offered. Production was scheduled to commence in two months. Joe had introduced personnel changes that made the operation more efficient and employees happier. The new marketing plan, rolled out three months earlier, had boosted sales significantly and held even greater promise for the future. Reports for the past two quarters revealed that for the first time in four years the company was in the black. They now even had sufficient resources to carry them through a slow period if one occurred. Above all, Joe had developed and was implementing a long-term strategy and a set of subsidiary ones covering the whole operation, which gave the board and employees confidence that the company's new direction was thoughtfully developed and would continue producing a profit.

Joe took satisfaction as well in knowing that he had met the expectations of his board. He sensed a high degree of satisfaction among employees also, emanating from working at a well-managed and successful company. In addition, Joe's quest to be the best possible CEO for the company had led him to optimize his personal life. He was now spending adequate time with his family and caring for his spiritual and physical health.

The Benefits of Living According to God's Design

Just as Joe experienced satisfaction resulting from ABC Widget Company running like a good company was designed to function, for many reasons we experience a profound sense of satisfaction as we succeed as CEO of our lives. We noted at the outset of this book that God designed us to function as agape-producing organisms. Just as a car runs well when we operate and maintain it according to the manufacturer's design, likewise all aspects of our lives function effectively as we maximize agape production.

Benefits to Others

The ultimate fulfillment resulting from maximum agape production resides in the benefit we are able to infuse into the lives of others. It is deeply rewarding to observe the impact on our spouse, children, co-workers, friends, people we have helped financially, and those to whom we have ministered in a variety of other ways. Knowing that their lives are better because of our influence elicits a large measure of joy. Joy that results from entertainment and other activities dissipates when the activity is finished. We can enjoy a great meal, but after we take the last bite the enjoyment is over. The joy that comes from displaying agape to others, however, comprises the gift that keeps on giving. The realization that we have blessed them provides a continuous fountain of fulfillment.

Personal Benefits

Agape production requires that we make every component of our life function optimally. As a result, by seeking to be our best for others, we become our best for ourselves. Living according to God's design blesses everyone. Below I list some salient areas in which we benefit.

Behavioral Benefits

Maximizing our agape output requires that all of our behaviors are moral, wise, disciplined, and gracious. This results in our behaving according to God design. Life is good when instead of DUIs and maxed out credit cards we are acting in godly, responsible ways, maintaining a lifestyle beneficial to all those whom our life touches.

Subjective Benefits

Optimal agape production also produces a profound sense of emotional well-being, eliminating feelings of irresponsibility and failure, shame and regret, and replacing them with the good conscience that results from living responsibly and effectively. But even more significant, a life characterized by agape production engenders emotional wellness because blessing others infuses joy and peace into the giver. In addition, we experience profound subjective fulfillment knowing that we are living according to God's instructions.

Relational Benefits

Pursuing optimal agape also produces wholesome relationships. It eliminates destructive relational interactions, replacing them with kindness, caring, and consideration. Seeking to be a blessing to our spouse, children, and others, also encourages a positive response from them, resulting in healthy and happy relationships.

Financial Benefits

Selfish living is expensive. We crave more than we can afford, and in addition, the devil pays poorly. A little sin can cost a lot of money. The agape-oriented life encourages financial responsibility and prudent use of money that promotes financial stability.

Physical Benefits

As we strategize to produce maximum agape, that process mandates care for our physical health. Maintaining our physical wellness enhances our capacity to display agape and the number of years across which we can produce it. Consequently, managing our lives to produce maximum agape results in optimizing our physical health.

Because we live in a fallen world, all of us encounter health issues. Nonetheless, living God's way minimizes those issues and maximizes our physical well-being.

Spiritual Benefits

Because the Holy Spirit serves as our business partner, we have ongoing interaction with Him in our moment by moment pursuit of agape production. This arrangement provides a major added dimension to our relationship with Him.

A marriage in which a husband and wife each does his or her own thing, interacting only in marriage-type activities, can be good. But one in which husband and wife share mutual objectives and continually work together to meet those objectives can be far richer. Studies reveal that people who work together on a project, who engage regularly in pursuit of a common goal, develop a powerful bond.

Likewise, when our relationship with the Lord is not confined to reading Scripture, praying, and worshiping, but also includes working together daily to achieve the success of Agape Incorporated, this arrangement makes that relationship far more dynamic and meaningful. This working together with the Lord appears to comprise the "abiding" type relationship to which Jesus calls us in John 15:4-7, a relationship in which our ongoing connection to the vine and the life that it supplies enables us to produce much fruit.

Eternal benefits

Not only does the production of maximum agape bring a full complement of benefits in this life, but it leads to rewards that will be a source of joy throughout all eternity.

The most profound benefit resulting from success as CEO of our lives resides in the joy of knowing that we have achieved God's purposes—lived lives pleasing to Him. It is difficult to imagine the overwhelming joy that we will experience when He says to us as He did to the servant earning 10 minas, "Well done, good and faithful servant." Whatever challenges we have faced and disciplines we have exercised to maximize agape, His commendation will make it worth it all.

As I discussed earlier, this life maintains such a strong grip on our thoughts and emotions that it is difficult for us to fully grasp the joys that eternal rewards will bring. Try as we might to maintain a spiritual perspective, we still retain an overblown estimation of this world's rewards. Only when we arrive in heaven will we fully appreciate the inestimable value of the eternal rewards that will be conferred on us for succeeding as CEO of our lives.

The Only Valid Definition of Success

This book has defined success based on God's definition,

that of maximum agape production. Might some other perspective on success be as good or even better? No. God's definition of success is the only valid one for many reasons.

First, in comparison to living for the benefit of God and fellow human beings, any other form of success rings hollow. Achievements of the rich and famous cannot hold a candle to it. Looking back over a life that honors God and that has blessed many people represents the ultimate success.

God's definition of success is the only genuine measure because ultimately He is the assessor and rewarder of success. In the long run, how others measure our success is irrelevant.

Producing maximum agape is also the ultimate measure of success because doing so fulfills our purpose for existence, the task for which we were designed as human beings.

Success according to God's design is also the ultimate measure because it embodies success that is not selfish. We succeed by benefitting others. Other types of success have self as the ultimate beneficiary and tend to trample others in their pursuit. Succeeding based on God's definition results in everyone winning.

Success is within Your Reach

I would like to conclude this book by revisiting a theme I emphasized toward its outset, that succeeding at life as described in this book is within the reach of each person. This assertion is not a cheesy, "You can be anything you want to be," graduation-speech-type cliché. Rather, success is a reality genuinely accessible to each one of us. God has given each of us a unique array of gifts that enables us to display optimal agape in the special situations in which He places us.

We live in a world in which caring people are becoming scarce. The deepening darkness gives greater visibility to the light produced by our agape. I once took my son trout fishing. We caught nothing. On the way home we stopped at a trout farm. We had much better success there. In our quest to show agape, our self-centered world has placed us on a trout farm. If we intentionally and aggressively pursue our mission of maximizing agape production, success is assured.

Funerals can be teachable events. They provide perspective on what matters in life. Solomon indicated that in the Book of Ecclesiastes by observing, "It is better to go to the house of mourning than to go to the house of feasting, for this is the end of all mankind, and the living will lay it to heart." (Ecclesiastes 7:2)

In recent years I have attended several funerals for individuals whom our society might categorize as common people. They nonetheless had produced uncommon legacies. Like Dorcas in Scripture, those observing their lives gave witness to the profuse trail of agape they had left behind, touching the lives of many people. I found those funerals especially challenging because they reminded me that God has placed success as CEO of our lives within reach of us all.

God has designed and called you to manage your life to produce maximum agape. He has provided you with all the resources necessary to achieve that objective. Through your partnership with the Holy Spirit and application of the principles described in this book, I have every confidence that you will succeed as CEO of your life.

Appendix A

Some Good News about the Most Important Trip You Will Ever Take

Seldom do we think of Jesus as a travel agent, but He does serve in that capacity, and as we might expect, He is the best ever.

The Destination

Unlike most travel agents, He only includes one destination in His offerings, which He describes in John 14:2, "In My Father's house are many mansions; if it were not so, I would have told you...." Here Jesus is telling us that the destination He offers is heaven. It doesn't get better than that.

Scripture describes this destination elsewhere, assuring us that heaven is a real place where we will enjoy many of the positive aspects of our present existence, only without any of the defects. Life in heaven does not consist of some surreal, floating-on-clouds type of existence. Rather, we will be fully engaged in normal human activities: eating, drinking, enjoying relationships, and participating in creative endeavors. Heaven won't seem like a strange environment, but rather we will immediately sense that we are finally home.

As the ultimate travel agent, in this verse Jesus tells us, "I go to prepare a place for you." He has already arrived at that destination to assure that all of the necessary preparations are being made for your arrival. You don't have to worry about encountering one of those experiences in which the receptionist says, "I don't see anyone by that name on my list." Nor will you need to worry about arriving at your new residence only to find that the contractor is behind schedule, and it will be a while until you can move in. You can be assured that Jesus will make preparations for your arrival beyond anything you ever imagined.

The Payment

The natural inclination is to ask, "How much will this trip cost?" This is where Jesus shines the brightest as the ultimate travel agent. In John 14:6 He explains, "I am the way, the truth, and the life. No one comes to the Father except through Me." In that verse, Jesus in essence is telling us that He has paid for our trip to heaven Himself, which He further explains in John 3:16, "For God so loved the world that He gave His only begotten Son, that whoever believes in Him should not perish but have everlasting life." This verse refers to God sending His Son, Jesus Christ, to earth to take on humanity and die on a cross to pay the penalty for our sins. In so doing, Jesus provides eternal life, that is, He covers our fare for the trip to heaven.

We might wonder why Jesus is paying the fare for us instead of making us pay. The answer is that we don't have the resources to pay. The Bible teaches that as sinful human beings we could never earn our way to heaven because any payment we might make would be tainted by sin and therefore not accepted for this trip. It would be like trying to use counterfeit money to pay for a plane ticket. The sacrifice made by Jesus of His death on the cross for our sins provides the only acceptable payment for this trip to heaven. That is why He paid for the trip Himself.

We might also question why Jesus would pay for our fare since the price was so high. The answer begins with the reality that because we are mortal beings, ultimately all of us are going to leave this earth headed for some place. Just as the destination planned by Jesus is the best we could ever imagine and beyond, there is only one alternative destination, and that one is far worse than anything that our minds could ever comprehend. Those not registered for the trip Jesus planned and paid for will by default head for that other terrible destination. This takes us to the ultimate reason for Jesus' willingness to pay our fare. Jesus' love for us compelled Him to provide an escape for us from that horrible eternal plight and instead to offer us passage to heaven—the ultimate alternative.

Some Good News about the Most Important Trip
You Will Ever Take

You Don't Have To Make the Trip Alone

One of the superior services extended by Jesus as the ultimate travel agent resides in His assurance that He will serve as our personal travel guide. In John 14:3 Jesus promises, "I will come again and receive you to Myself; that where I am, there you may be also." As the time approaches for us to depart for this trip to heaven, we may feel a degree of anxiety over leaving our present, familiar surroundings and heading for an unfamiliar destination. In the passage above we find Jesus assuring us that when our departure time arrives we will not have to make that trip alone, but that He will make the journey with us, assuring us of His company until we have become settled in at our wonderful new destination.

How to Sign Up for the Trip

Since heaven constitutes the ultimate destination, since the alternative is so terrible, and since Jesus has already paid the fare and will make the trip with us, you might be wondering how to sign up. We find the answer in John 3:16, already quoted above. That verse tells us that "whoever believes in Him will not perish but have everlasting life." That term "believes" can be confusing because it has several different meanings. A good way to understand its use in this verse is found in the analogy of marriage. The traditional wedding vows, after the couple in effect pledges their lives to each other, end with the statement, "And thereto I pledge you my faith." In this context the term "faith" is referring to the commitment just made in the vows. Marriage requires a major commitment. It calls us to leave our previous independent, self-directed life in which we could live as we pleased, and to commit ourselves to a new life in which seeking the welfare of another person become the primary consideration.

This metaphor gives us a vivid picture of the nature of biblical faith, the faith needed to receive eternal life, to register for the trip to heaven. That faith calls us to repent, i.e. abandon our old self-directed approach to life and commit ourselves to a relationship with Jesus, which includes our willingness to live under His authority and seek to please Him.

One might wonder whether this commitment to live for Jesus doesn't comprise our paying part of the fare. This perspective is wrong because living for Jesus does not constitute a price we pay but a benefit that we receive. Our lives are not worse but far better when lived on His terms.

Scripture describes this existence as eternal life, which refers both to the duration of this life and also its quality. This eternal life begins as soon as one makes that commitment to Jesus. Though receiving eternal life does not make our current existence heaven on earth, life does take on a heavenly quality as we live in fellowship with Christ and as He empowers us to reflect His character. Though the trip to heaven is future, the benefits begin now.

Signing Up

We discussed signing up for this journey by means of a faith commitment to Jesus Christ. You might wonder how you do that.

I already mentioned the marriage metaphor. Establishing a relationship with Jesus Christ is somewhat like saying wedding vows. Jesus said His vows to you almost 2000 years ago when He gave His life on the cross, signifying that He made payment in full for your sins with the words, "It is finished." You can complete the transaction by saying your vows to Him, by in your own words telling Him that because He gave His life to pay for your sins, you are committing your life to Him.

Jesus will respond to your vows by forgiving your sins, imparting eternal life to you, living in fellowship with you, and empowering you to live according to His Word. As you walk in fellowship with Him during this life, moving from this life to the next will become a transition as natural as taking a journey with a friend.

Jesus is the ultimate travel agent because He has prepared the ultimate destination, paid for the trip, and will take the journey with you. I hope you will sign up for this trip today.

Appendix B
My Package of Gifts for Producing Agape

Spiritual gifts

Gift	How much (On a Scale of 1-10)	Description

Natural gifts

Gift	How much (On a Scale of 1-10)	Description

Other resources:

Type	How much (On a Scale of 1-10)	Description
Finances		
Possessions		
Education and certifications		
Positions		
Marriage and family		
Business and social network		
Other		

Dr. Brownback is available to present this material in seminars. He can be contacted at pbrownback@gmail.com

Endnotes

[i] Eckblad, John; Eckblad, John; Kiel, David; Kiel, David (2003-02-22). *If Your Life Were a Business, Would You Invest In It? The 13-Step Program for Managing Your Life Like the Best CEO's Manage Their Companies* (Page v). McGraw-Hill Education. Kindle Edition.

[ii] Ibid. Kindle Edition.

[iii] http://lemonsmile.tumblr.com

[iv] https://en.wikipedia.org/wiki/Jerry_Rice

[v] https://quotefancy.com/quote/50164/Jerry-Rice-Today-i-will-do-what-others-won-t-so-tomorrow-i-can-do-what-others-can-t

[vi] https://www.profootballhof.com/players/jerry-rice/

[vii] https://wilbrewer.wordpress.com/2013/05/24/are-you-a-victim-of-delegating-up/

[viii] Commentary notes on Romans 8:15. Vincent, M.R.– Word Studies in the New Testament, e-Sword 11.1.0 edition.

[ix] Commentary notes on Galatians 4:5. Walvoord, John F. and Zuck, Roy B.– The Bible Knowledge Commentary, e-Sword 11.1.0 edition.

[x] Davis, Dale. *Draw Me Nearer*: p. 153.

[xi] Johnson, Paul, *A History of the American People*: New York, NY: Harper Collins Publishers, 1997.

[xii] https://www.youtube.com/watch?v=E8HffdyLdoc

[xiii] Elliot, Elisabeth, *Through Gates of Splendor*: Tyndale House, 1986.

[xiv] https://interestingengineering.com/what-are-gyroscopes-and-why-are-they-important

Made in the USA
Columbia, SC
07 March 2019